Building a
DISCIPLE-
MAKING
MINISTRY

The Timeless Principles of Arthur Flake
for Sunday School and Small Groups

Compiled by
Ken Braddy and Allan Taylor

© 2020 Lifeway Press

Reprinted August 2021

Additional helps available online at
www.lifeway.com/trainingresources.

ISBN 978-1-0877-4491-9

Item 005831915

Dewey decimal classification: 268.0

Subject headings: SUNDAY SCHOOLS/RELIGIOUS
EDUCATION

Unless otherwise noted, all Scripture quotations are taken from the
Christian Standard Bible, © 2017 by Holman Bible Publishers.

Used by permission.

Printed in United States

Contents

Preface

Pandemic. Masks. Social distancing. Sickness. Death. Fear. Uncertainty. The thought of a worldwide pandemic and the interruption of the American economy occupied the forefront of news outlets. Millions of people worldwide contracted a deadly virus, and they died. Hundreds of thousands of Americans, in spite of their best efforts to protect themselves, contracted the deadly disease and died, too. And no, I'm not talking about COVID-19 and the year 2020.

I am speaking of the Spanish Flu, a terrible pandemic that affected the world almost exactly 100 years ago. From 1918–1919, news of the Spanish Flu could be found on the front pages of newspapers around the world. No one could escape its influence. Not even the Sunday School Board of the Southern Baptist Convention.

The work of producing trustworthy Sunday School resources for the church ground to a halt. Workers were sent home. Orders that originated from Southern Baptist churches for curriculum ceased. Financial strains put enormous pressure on the Southern Baptist Convention's publishing agency. The Sunday School Board (now Lifeway Christian Resources), fought for its survival. And survive it did.

As the country began to emerge from the Spanish Flu pandemic, the Southern Baptist Convention gathered in Georgia in the spring of 1919. Within the pages of the many reports given by Sunday School Board leaders to the attendees of that year's annual meeting we find words that give us a glimpse of how the country, the church, and the Sunday School Board began to emerge from a terrible chapter in American history.

> *At the very time of greatest stress came the epidemic of influenza, and this was perhaps the most far-reaching hindrance to Sunday-school work which has been known in a generation... The influence of the epidemic stayed with us through December, but the bright sun-shiny months of the opening year gave reassurance. Our Sunday Schools rallied, business became more normal, conditions improved, and the working force of the Board*

resumed its normal operations. We had anticipated that it would take many months for the Sunday Schools to rally, but they came back in March. There flowed in a steady stream of orders, which indicated that the Sunday-school hosts were well organized, full of purpose, and had rallied themselves. As a result, the year, which had been so trying for many months, ended full of hope and promise." (Annual of the Southern Baptist Convention 1919, pp.449-450)

As the country emerged from a global pandemic in 1919, one of its employees, Mr. Arthur Flake, was asked to lead the new Sunday School department. In the years that followed the Spanish Flu pandemic, Arthur Flake became a prolific writer. He encouraged churches to reach people with the gospel. He was a strong proponent of training workers. He wrote books and made speeches and presentations around the country. And people listened.

During his time at the Sunday School Board, Arthur Flake developed a strategy for growing the Sunday School. We know it today as "Flake's Formula." It is a simple five-step formula for growing a church's disciple-making ministry. It is the subject of this book.

My friend Allan Taylor, a well-known Sunday School advocate, believed it was necessary to tell Arthur Flake's story and to demonstrate that although this man's life and ministry took place at a different time, the principles he espoused are still effective today. A number of Christian educators were recruited to write the chapters in this book, and we find it interesting that today we face a similar pandemic 100 years later. And we are asking the same questions that Arthur Flake and Christian leaders asked in 1919: "How do we make disciples in the world in which we live?"

COVID-19. When this book was first imagined, that word was not in our vocabulary. In the months that followed the writing of the chapters in this book, that word came to prominence in national and local news, magazines, and the internet. A once-thriving economy ground to a halt. Churches moved to online worship and giving. Bible study groups learned how to take advantage of the digital technologies that allowed them to meet online even though they were separated and sequestered in an attempt to flatten the curve of the COVID-19 virus.

Our hope is that you will be encouraged by the story of Arthur Flake, and that you will embrace his simple five-step formula for growing your church's disciple-making ministry.

I'd like to acknowledge the help and contributions of the First Baptist Church of Winona, Mississippi. It was this church where Arthur Flake served as director of Sunday School. The congregation functioned as the lab in which Flake's formula was tested and imagined, and we are indebted to them for doing so. The pastor, Brother Jay Anderson, met with me, as did one of his key lay leaders, Dr. Tom Dulin. These two men were invaluable in helping me know things about Arthur Flake that I could not have known otherwise.

Ken Braddy
Director of Sunday School

Introduction

This book is about a great man, Arthur Flake. Flake is the patriarch of Southern Baptist Sunday School. Flake came to the Sunday School Board as a field agent and ascended to the role of the Board's first Secretary of the Department of Sunday School Administration in 1920.

You may be asking, "Why would I want to read about a man and his ministry that took place 100 years ago?" I'm glad you asked.

First, Flake was used mightily of God to take the ministry of Sunday School to new heights. People love to read about great and influential men. Libraries are filled with exciting biographies of those who have impacted the world, politics, medicine, sports, and religion. Although this book is not a biography, it will highlight the life of a great man that you will enjoy getting to know.

Secondly, this is a great read on leadership. Leadership matters. The need for great leaders in our churches today is enormous. Leaders are the designers of our ministries. As a great architect, Flake drafted a blueprint that launched the church into an era of building tremendous Bible teaching, gospel-sharing Sunday Schools.

Thirdly, the principles he taught and practiced were effective in his day and are still viable today. Keith Kenemer, my friend and retired Church Ministries Consultant has often reminded me of Flake's Formula (chapters 3-7) with this statement, "Methods are many, principles are few; methods may change, principles never do!

This book has a two-fold purpose. First, 2020 is the year of Arthur Flake's 100th anniversary of becoming the first Sunday School Secretary of the Baptist Sunday School Board in Nashville, Tennessee (now called LifeWay). We want to commemorate and celebrate this great leader whose impact is still felt today.

Secondly, we want to revisit his Sunday School growth principles and see how they still are applicable to us today. The study of history should always have a place in society because history gives perspective. As a boy I was required to study my state history and the history of our country. Mission teams often study the background of the foreign country in which they will minister so they will have an understanding of the people and culture. In his New Testament writings, the Apostle Paul often referred to the Old Testament. On the occasion of writing to the church at Corinth he wanted them to be aware and reminded of an incident that occurred as the Israelites were wandering for forty years before entering the promised land (1 Corinthians 10:1-13). He concluded by writing, "These things happened to them as examples, and they were written for our instruction ..." (v. 10).[1] The feast of Passover was to be observed every year so the Hebrews would always keep in mind the perspective of God's great deliverance. Perspective makes us wiser and more effective. This book will give you a historical perspective that translates into effective, modern day practices.

Great men who practiced the principles Flake taught wrote this book. I know all these men personally. They are not just philosophers who talk about Flake's principles; they are men who have practiced his principles. These men have dedicated their lives raising up Sunday Schools that are committed to make disciples by reaching people, teaching people, and ministering to people (Matthew 4:23; 9:35; 28:19-20)

If you want to make disciples, reach lost and unchurched people, have people learning Scripture, and serving others, then read this book! Remember, methods are many, principles are few; methods may change; principles never do!

Allan Taylor

CHAPTER 1

Who was Arthur Flake?

Ken Braddy

Texan

Arthur Flake is best known as a famous Sunday School leader in the Southern Baptist Convention during the early to mid-1900s. In trying to describe Mr. Flake, some have applied the term "pioneer" to him. "If vision, courage, clarity of purpose, and abundance of energy are attributes of the pioneer, then he has been one."[3] Mr. Flake was born on November 17, 1862, to A.J. and Lucinda Catherine (Burroughs). His father was from Mississippi, and his mother was from South Carolina. Arthur Flake was born on the Texas prairie at a site that is now present-day Temple, Texas.[4]

Flake grew up in the small town of LaGrange, Texas, a city located in Fayette County, in the middle of the triangle formed between San Antonio, Houston, and Austin, Texas. Established around 1828, the city of LaGrange had a population of approximately 2,400 persons according to the census of 1900. The city was situated at a bend in the Colorado River. Surrounded by a bluff and a high plateau, the city was sheltered on all sides against storms, and was a favorite campground of native Americans who liked settling in storm-proof locations. When Arthur Flake was just five years old, the city of LaGrange suffered an outbreak of Yellow Fever, and a few years after that it experienced a devastating flood.[5]

Mr. Flake's family relocated from Fayette County to Bell County, Texas, about 130 miles to the northwest of LaGrange. He attended schools in Bell County, Texas. He spent a busy boyhood working on his family's farm, and then became a clerk at a dry goods store; he went on to attend the South Belton Institute. Although he attended public schools, Mr. Flake was known to laughingly say from time to time that he "finished in the university of Plug and Dig."[6] For five years Arthur Flake traveled across Texas, working for a Louisville,

Kentucky clothing firm. He moved on to work for a different clothing company; his territories included Louisiana, Mississippi, Alabama, Tennessee, and Arkansas. After nine years of being a traveling salesman, Flake was ready for a change of pace.[7]

Arthur Flake soon turned his sights eastward, moving to Mississippi to pursue business opportunities. But the real turning point in his life came at age 31 when he attended a revival in Meridian, Mississippi. It was here that Arthur Flake gave his life to Christ at the Cumberland Presbyterian Church.[8] His new relationship with Jesus would prove pivotal to the life journey he was traveling.

Entrepreneur

Flake relocated to Winona, Mississippi, a small town in north central Mississippi, approximately halfway between Memphis, Tennessee, and Jackson, Mississippi. The town of Winona was at the crossroads of the state, with three U.S. highways converging there. In 1894, Arthur Flake decided to enter into the department store business at the age of thirty-two. Centrally located in the state, the city of Winona promised to be fertile ground in which to plant a business. His new retail clothing store became a success. He would continue along this path for fifteen years.

Lay Church Leader

Within one year of moving to Winona, Mississippi, Arthur Flake joined the First Baptist Church of Winona and formed what is believed to be the first Training Union in the state of Mississippi, which was the Baptist Young People's Union (B.Y.P.U.). "In 1895 he founded the first B.Y.P.U. in the state and gained a reputation as an inspired speaker and church builder."[9] There was another reason 1895 was an important year for Arthur Flake, because it was on June 16 he married Miss Lena Nelson at Baldwyn, Mississippi.[10] In time, three daughters would be born to Flake and his wife: Katherine, Mildred, and Marjorie. In 1896, Flake began his Sunday School career, becoming superintendent of his local Sunday School, continuing in that role until 1909.[11]

Mr. Flake was open to being used by the Lord as a layman in his church. On the heels of his recent conversion to Christ, he became a powerful example of what God can do when His people willingly serve and use their spiritual gifts in the local church. Flake's story is also an encouraging example, because if God can use an ordinary person like Arthur Flake, how might He also use you and me to do similar things for God in our churches?

Evangelist

In 1899, Arthur Flake helped organize the Mississippi State B.Y.P.U. Convention, and served as president until 1903. Unbeknownst to Flake at this time, his passion for reaching young people with the gospel would soon lead to new opportunities at the Sunday School Board of the Southern Baptist Convention in Nashville, Tennessee. His sphere of influence was about to expand exponentially. Because of his success in organizing young people and creating processes to help them grow as disciples, and because of his tireless work in his state's convention on their behalf, he would soon be invited to become part of the Southern Baptist Convention's new Sunday School Board so that he could expand the ministry to young people everywhere. [12]

Sunday School Man

As a Mississippi layman, "He was chairman of the state committee to select L.P. Leavell as the first Sunday school secretary in Mississippi, and Mr. Leavell in turn persuaded Mr. Flake to leave his clothing business and move to Nashville with the Sunday School Board in 1909 ...." [13] By 1908, the Sunday School growth at the First Baptist Church of Winona, Mississippi, caught the attention of leaders at the fledgling Sunday School Board, as did Flake's passion for reaching young people with the gospel through the BYPU ministry. Now forty-seven, Mr. Flake had become a seasoned Sunday School growth agent and a disciple-maker. After meeting with Sunday School Board leaders in Memphis, Tennessee to discuss a leadership position with the Board, Flake accepted a position offered to him by J.M. Frost, president of the Sunday School Board. In a letter to Dr. Frost dated April 30, 1908, regarding a meeting held between them in Memphis, Tennessee, to discuss the particulars of a position at the Sunday School Board, Arthur Flake said the following:

Dear Dr. Frost,

Regarding our conference in Memphis a week ago, I beg to say that I have not yet reached a decision in the matter, and it will take considerable time for me to do so. It may be that I can transfer my mercantile business to a different management, and as I said, I expect to shift the responsibility of the Water & Light Plant at an early date. There are yet many things in the way. I know that my desire is to enter more actively into the Lord's work than I have done here-to-before, and this opportunity which seems to be clearly of the Lord, appeals to me strongly, and I am free to say I want to do the work. The need of the BYPU weights on my heart heavily, more especially as I see interests in the work wane among its friends. In my opinion a revival of interests will be more easily enlisted since the Sunday School Board is going to get behind the movement ... I long to go into the work and hope to be able to do so. I beg to express my appreciation of the conference with you and the other brethren in Memphis. It helped me. My expenses to Memphis were $8.65. [14]

It is clear from this letter that Arthur Flake was thinking deeply about joining the Sunday School Board, getting out of the mercantile business, and devoting his life to the Lord's work on a full-time basis. By 1909, Flake had accepted Dr. Frost's offer to serve at the Sunday School Board. Flake's role was that of field agent. His new work meant that he would focus on providing leadership to the BYPU (Baptist Young People's Union). For the next several years, he would set aside his passion for Sunday School and focus on the BYPU, but he never left his first love. Little did he know it, but in just a few more years, he would land the position of a lifetime, one that would take him back into the world of Sunday School. But that position would not be with the Sunday School Board. In fact, Arthur Flake was on a pathway that would lead him back to his native Texas—temporarily.

Sunday School Board Leader

After serving as a field agent for ten years, strengthening the work of the BYPU, Arthur Flake resigned his position at the Sunday School Board. In 1919 he went back to his home state of Texas to assume a leadership role at the First Baptist Church of Forth Worth. The pastor of the church, the controversial and outspoken fundamentalist preacher J. Frank Norris, hired Flake to be in charge of all church organizations and activities. Although he did not have the official title, Flake essentially became one of the earliest ministers of education in Southern Baptist churches. Flake had a big job on his hands, because membership in the Sunday School of First Baptist Church Fort Worth was more than four thousand. The new job returned Flake to his passion—Sunday School ministry. He had grown weary of the required travel with his position at the Sunday School Board, and he truly wanted to focus on Sunday School and not the BYPU ministry. However, after just a few months, it was apparent to him that the new position at First Baptist Fort Worth was not going to work out. "Flake decided Pastor Norris was too tough to work with, left First Church Fort Worth, and moved back to Nashville and the Board. He was appointed secretary of the new Sunday School Administration Department where, at the age of fifty-eight, he began his most enduring work."[15] This time, there would be no going back to Texas. Arthur Flake's life and ministry now centered around his work in Nashville, Tennessee, and he made growing, strengthening, and improving Sunday School the focus of the rest of his life.

"The Formula Man"

Arthur Flake made significant contributions to the Southern Baptist Convention and to the ministry of Sunday School during his second time at the Sunday School Board. After assuming his duties as the head of the Sunday School department, he published his first book, *Building a Standard Sunday School,* in 1922. He went on to develop the contribution he is most remembered for—"Flake's Formula." With considerable experience in the local church, Flake was able to compress Sunday School work into five essential steps. These steps formed the basis of his five-step formula for growing and expanding the Sunday school. "According to Landrum Leavell, the formula increased attendance in Flake's Winona Sunday School by 500 percent."[16]

In the early 1900s, there was considerable focus on Scientific Management Theory as a means of increasing the efficiency of companies and organizations by prescribing certain steps that were repeatable. It's popularity led people to apply its principles to all segments of society, including the church. Scientific Management Theory (SMT) was seen as the way to get results during a pragmatic time in America's history and industrialization. During the early 1900s, "Arthur Flake ... advocated application of the theory's principles to education within the church."[17] Frederick Taylor published his Scientific Management Theory in 1911, just as Arthur Flake was beginning his first role at the Sunday School Board. By the time Flake left the board and returned in 1920, SMT had grown in popularity for almost a decade. Flake applied the principles to Sunday School, and "Flake's Formula" was born.

Trainer

Arthur Flake traveled and trained leaders to grow and expand their Sunday Schools through the implementation of his five-step process. Flake was a dynamic speaker, and was always in demand. He was quick to share the good news of his increasingly popular five-step formula. "He went all over the Southern Baptist Convention preaching his gospel of 'The Five Steps in Building a Great Sunday School.' Again and again he said: 'You can build a great Sunday School anywhere if you will do these five things: (1) Know your possibilities; (2) enlarge your organization; (3) make a place for the people; (4) train teachers and officers (5) go after them."[18] Flake's affect on the communities in which Southern Baptist churches existed was immediate. Enthusiasm for his formula for growing Sunday School led churches to conduct door-to-door censuses; people who had been left alone by religious organizations suddenly found themselves being confronted by well-meaning church members who were searching for lost souls unconnected to the church. These unchurched families were enrolled in Sunday School and churches experienced the blessings of their work: baptisms moved upward, as did attendance and financial giving.

Editor & Author

As if this weren't enough, Flake was not content to sit on his laurels. As the director of the department of Sunday School, he established *The Sunday School Builder*, a monthly magazine on Sunday School organization and administration of which he served as editor. He was adamant that his new Sunday School Department provide free leaflets on all aspects of Sunday School administration. At one time, the department provided upwards of seventy-five pamphlets for all aspects of Sunday School work. "Later, the material in these leaflets was expanded and completed and put into a series of textbooks which are absolutely without equal in this field. These books have become the guiding standard for our Sunday School organization and promotion. They are recognized by many denominations and have been translated into several languages."[19] The author of *Baptist Leaders in Religious Education* noted that at one time, he wrote to Arthur Flake for help in creating a growing Sunday School. Mr. Flake sent a package of the leaflets produced by his department, the writer followed the advice in them, and the Sunday School grew from 442 to an average of nearly 800 in just one year.[20]

Flake wrote almost a dozen books after he was fifty-eight years old! It is estimated that over a million people have read his books and been influenced by his thinking. He wrote his final book, *Life at 80 As I See It*, in 1944; he implored adults to continue serving the Lord and to remain active in living out their faith. The dedication page of this final work of Arthur Flake says, "To all old people generally…and to all who desire earnestly to make their lives more beautiful and useful as they grow old."[21] The first chapter sums up the gist of the book: "Deeds, Not Years, Make up Life."

Growth & Change Agent

During this golden age of Sunday School growth, God blessed the work of Arthur Flake and the men and women of the Sunday School Board. During these years, considerable things took place to advance Sunday School throughout the churches of the Southern Baptist Convention:

- *Scores of new teachers and officers were enlisted*
- *Classes were divided*
- *Prospective students were assigned*
- *New departments were formed*
- *Week-long growth campaigns added hundreds of people at a time*
- *Church buildings were taxed to capacity*
- *Classes met in auditoriums, separated by curtains and screens*
- *Groups met in schools, nearby businesses, stores, and residences*
- *Old buildings were remodeled and enlarged*
- *New buildings were erected*[22]

During his era of providing Sunday School leadership at the Board, Flake also "had much to do with 'discovering' Harold Ingraham, J.N. Barnette, and other Sunday school leaders." He raised up contemporaries, and he raised up future leaders who would champion Sunday School and its place in Southern Baptist life long after he had retired from the work he was called to so many years before.

Flake's contributions to the growth of the Southern Baptist Convention are not in dispute. Few men have the singular impact of Arthur Flake. His formula has endured the test of time and has been used by many denominations, and by churches in all parts of the country. Perhaps one of his most important contributions as a growth agent was to help people see Sunday School as something for every person, not just children. Flake was convinced that every person should have the opportunity to study the Bible—both Christians and the spiritually lost. "A major factor in the evangelistic work of the Southern Baptist Convention was Sunday School work, for it made Sunday School the overarching program of the church, touching all other aspects of a church's programs. Flake also helped convince the Convention about the value of Sunday School as a tool for evangelism. When the Sunday School movement in general began to emphasize nurture more than witness, Southern Baptists continued to perceive Sunday School as the outreach arm of the church."[23]

Good and Faithful Servant

Arthur Flake requested retirement from the Sunday School Board in 1936. He began living his retirement days with one of his three daughters, Miss Mildred Flake, in Memphis, Tennessee, at 1505 Linden Avenue. She provided care for him during his retirement years.[24] On July 3, 1952, Arthur Flake died in Memphis, Tennessee, at ninety years old. His funeral brought together many Southern Baptists, including Dr. Robert G. Lee and Harold Ingraham, who officiated his funeral. Harold Ingraham said of Flake after his death, "He taught Southern Baptists how to build Sunday schools, and this teaching has been basic in bringing our Sunday school enrolment (sic) from around one million in 1910 to nearly six million in 1952."[25]

Conclusion

The life of Arthur Flake demonstrates that one man can truly make a difference. The church and Sunday School would be much different today had Arthur Flake not had the influence he did over the church's most important ministry—Sunday School. People who knew him best have said:

- *"Arthur Flake…developed a simple plan that was enough dynamite to blow up the Sunday School world and rebuild it on new lines"* – Sunday School Board historian P.E. Burroughs.

- *"Flake's Formula is the skeleton on which everything else hangs"* – A.V. Washburn, Secretary of the Sunday School Department.[26]

Chuck Kelley, president emeritus of New Orleans Baptist Theological Seminary, wrote the following about Flake's influence in Southern Baptist life in his book, *Fuel The Fire*:

"The success of Arthur Flake was no fluke. Nearly all Southern Baptist Sunday School strategies are variations or elaborations of his philosophy of Sunday school. Southern Baptists found that, with Flake's principles, Sunday School can be an extremely effective vehicle for evangelism and church growth. What made Sunday School such an important part of the evangelism process? If lost and unchurched prospects could get connected to a Sunday School class, two important things would happen over time. First, they would hear more and more of the Bible explained. The gospel would become more familiar and better understood. Second, the lost and unchurched would have natural opportunities to form relationships with Christians in the class and church. Such relationships often proved crucial in nurturing faith."[27]

Does Sunday school still work? The answer is yes. The caveat is that you must work Sunday School. Perhaps a solemn warning from A.V. Washburn would be appropriate here. Maybe this sums up the current state of Sunday School in the Southern Baptist Convention and beyond, or the Sunday School at your church: "Over the years, we lost the emphasis on evangelism that was basic to Flake's Formula because of the temptation to try some new things that get away from Flake's basics."[28] May this book remind us of the great heritage we have as Southern Baptists with regard to the Sunday School. May this book also challenge and inspire us to return to the basics of outreach, evangelism, training, and enlargement of our Sunday School organizations. In a day and time when there is "nothing new under the sun," may we find our roots and return to the basics that are essential for making disciples, so that old things are new again.

CHAPTER 2

Arthur Flake's Journal

Dwayne McCrary

In the entrance to LifeWay's headquarters in Nashville, Tennessee, is a display case. Inside this case is the journal of Arthur Flake. People pass by the case daily without truly understanding the importance of the journal they see inside. Flake's journal contains the outline for what would later become his first book, *Building a Standard Sunday School*. Contained within the pages of that journal are strategic actions based on Flake's deeply held beliefs that can help churches reach people for Christ. Some of Flake's insights contained in his journal never made it into print. Some of those unpublished portions provide deep insights into best practices we should lead our churches to embrace, and the reasons why we should do so.

To clarify, Arthur Flake's notes are not in what we might call a "journal" today. Flake recorded his notes in a copy of the 1918 edition of *The New Convention Normal Manual for Sunday School Workers* (first printed in 1913 with B.W. Spilman serving as the editor). Don't let the title confuse you. A "normal school" was a term used in those days for a school dedicated to training teachers. Today, many colleges and universities, some of which began as "normal schools" (UCLA, Eastern Michigan, San Jose State, Indiana State, and Sam Houston State, just to name a few), continue training teachers as a part of their purpose.

The manual was designed to train all Sunday School leaders and was divided into three sections: (1) the Sunday School (the big picture actions and administration, written by B.W Spilman), (2) the Pupil (teaching principles for different age groups, written by L.P. Leavell), and (3) the Bible (a survey of the Old and New Testament, written by P. E. Burroughs). Blank pages separated each section, and Flake filled those pages with his ideas. Much like you and I might do, Flake read the content in each section, and then wrote his own ideas in response. The comments in the margins and the hand-written notes give us insight into the thoughts and ideas behind what became known as Flake's Formula.

Finding His Why

The pages most people turn to first when handed Flake's journal are the two pages on which he wrote the initial proposal for mobilizing a Sunday School to reach the community, that eventually became Flake's Formula. A photo of these pages can be found in the Addendum (p. 123). On the top left quarter of these two facing pages, Flake wrote and underlined a simple statement: "All need it—all need to study the Bible."

Sunday School began to lose its way in the early 1900s. Some began to focus on adult groups and ignore children. Others focused on believers, missing the opportunity to involve the unchurched and unaffiliated. Others focused more on gathering people just like them and ignored others with different ethnic, economic, and social backgrounds. "All" was a radical idea in 1920 as America recovered from the Spanish Flu, a post war economy, and social unrest.

Under Flake's note about everyone needing to study the Bible, Flake wrote: "people who do not go to Sunday school do not study Bible." Flake connected individual Bible study with participation in a group Bible study. Being in a healthy Bible study group holds us accountable for studying beyond the group, on our own. The most common metaphor used in the Bible to describe God's people is the word "sheep." Sheep need to eat every day, and Christians need spiritual nourishment every day, too. Unless our Bible study group meets every day, then we must learn to feed ourselves.

Ideally, we study before the group time to prepare to participate in the group discussion, or we study after the group time to dig deeper into the truths introduced during the group time, or we do both. The issue is not so much about whether we prepare or study in response, but that we engage with the Bible every day. Flake understood the value of Bible study in a group and for individuals. Both are affirmed in his notes and one is seen as supporting the other.

Arthur Flake's desire was to give everyone in a local church's ministry context the opportunity to study the Bible. Flake viewed everything through that lens. As he studied scientific management theory, he did so through the lens of building a Sunday School that reached communities with the gospel. He was not the first to apply management theory to the Sunday School, he was just the one who was able to print it in a popular form. Some criticized him for using "secular" means when dealing with sacred topics, but his "why" was stronger than his opponent's criticism.

Since the notes in Flake's copy of *The New Convention Normal Manual for Sunday School Workers* served as the basis of his 1922 book *Building a Standard Sunday School*, we can examine what was ultimately printed to get a sense of what he valued.

Flake organized his original thoughts regarding the actions needed for reaching a community through the Sunday School into five actions. These actions were:

1. Find out who should belong;
2. Assort, grade, and tabulate;
3. Enlarge the organization;
4. Grade the Sunday School; and
5. Go after them.

What made it into print in Flake's 1922 book reads differently. Even the title for this group of actions was changed. In his notes, Flake had classified these actions and titled them *Enrollment*, but in the 1922 book he titled them *Enlargement*. Here are the actions Flake included in his 1922 book:

I. The Constituency for the Sunday School Should Be Known;
II. The Organization Should Be Enlarged;
III. A Suitable Place Should Be Provided;
IV. The Enlarged Organization Should Be Set Up; and
V. A Program of Visitation Should Be Maintained. [29]

Within these five items, we can see the original ideas from the notes. *Assort, grade,* and *tabulate* was absorbed into the *The Constituency for the Sunday School Should Be Known* action. *Grade the Sunday School* was included in *The Organization Should Be Enlarged.* He added *The Enlarged Organization Should Be Set Up* as a way to emphasize the need for what we might call promotion or launch day. *Providing suitable space* was an addition found in other sections of Flake's handwritten notes. *Go after them* was given a new name, reflecting the focus of Flake's explanation in the handwritten notes. Seeing the differences gives us some insight into the editorial process. Can you imagine the conversations that took place from the day Flake presented his notes to the editorial team and the day the book went to print?

Along the way, the actions found in his notes and the 1922 book took on new titles which became synonymous with Flake. They are:

1. **Know** the possibilities;
2. **Enlarge** the Organization;
3. **Enlist** and train leaders;
4. **Provide** space and resources; and
5. **Go** after the people.

Authorities debate when he actually presented his plan in this five-point format. They have proposed various theories, the most common being that these actions were the talking points of a "stump speech" or the session topics of a Sunday School revival or clinic presented by Flake. The truth is, we do not know when Flake first stated his plan in these specific five points or in what context. Regardless, these became the elements that Christian educators clung to as they built effective Sunday Schools. (See Appendix for Chart: Genesis of Flake's Formula, p. 105.)

As one researches the genesis of Flake's Formula, one will find the formula in various orders. All renditions begin with "Know the possibilities" and end with "Go after the people." The middle three is where we will find the varaince. Some list "Enlist and Train" as the second action with "Enlarge the Organization" as the third action. These lists tend to emphasize enlisting as an ongoing action and therefore taking place earlier in the process. In this approach, people are enlisted as potential leaders and prepared for a future yet-to-be determined responsibility. This may also reflect the fourth action defined in the 1922 book as "The Enlarged Organization should be Set Up" (was identified as "Grade the Sunday School" in his notes). Most would call this action launch day or promotion day as described in the notes and 1922 book (the first day the new organization is actually in place and functioning) which carries a different understanding than what is typically identified as enlarging the organization.

Some lists place "Enlarge" as the second action, "Provide space and resources" as the third action, and "Enlist" as the fourth action. These lists emphasize the value of recruiting someone to a specific task and sharing with them the curriculum they will be using and location in which they will be leading when approaching them to serve.

Other lists follow the pattern followed by this book: *Enlarge, Enlist, Provide*. Flake's notes combined enlarge and enlist as one action which adds to the debate as to which comes first. The way these were organized in Building a Standard Sunday School follows the same pattern as the notes. He used the term *Enlarge* to define the step and then the bulk of his notes were about enlisting leaders and teachers. However the first part of his comments under this section of his notes and in the 1922 book point to a Sunday School not growing because they are the same size year over year. Flake also defined this enlarge action in terms of adding to the organization based on who was discovered in step one (know the possibilities). The order followed in this book reflects how his notes were organized at that point.

To be true to the process identified by Flake in his notes and the 1922 book, the following steps might better reflect his thoughts:

- *Know the possibilities;*
- *Enlarge the organization;*
- *Enlist and train;*
- *Provide space and resources;*
- *Launch the new organization; and*
- *Go after the people.*

So why bring this up? When we compare his original notes to what made it into print in a book carrying his name, we get the idea that Flake was more concerned about having people involved in Bible study than he was about the semantics of a plan. A margin note helps us understand this better. On page 14 of his copy of *The New Convention Normal Manual* (which was an overview of the section on grading), Flake wrote across the top of the page, "not because of mental attainment, but because of spiritual need." Grading for Flake was about more than simply regrouping people on an annual basis. His idea of grading centered on creating new groups. The proposed plan, what we call "Flake's Formula," was to be a set of actions performed annually that led to relaunching, regrouping, and creating new groups.

His margin notes and underlining of the content in his copy of *The New Convention Normal Manual* reveal that Flake saw this spiritual need in at least two ways. First of all, he saw this spiritual need in developmental terms. How you communicate with a 4-year-old is different than how you communicate with a 40-year-old. He was an advocate for age-based learning that took into account the developmental needs of the learner.

Secondly, he understood this need in terms of salvation. "Grading" people was about making room for others who had yet to hear the gospel. That need grew every year as new people were discovered (enrolled), moved into the community, or were born. A grading/grouping chart served as a snapshot of an identified community with a growing spiritual need.

Identifying for the Challenges

As noted, Flake faced criticism and challenges. As a person who led Sunday School in the local church for several years, he knew from experience the challenges and obstacles that would lie ahead for the Sunday School leader.

On page 17 of *The New Convention Normal Manual,* Spilman stated, "Sunday schools which enjoy the luxury of graded buildings find no difficulty in maintaining the grade and department lines.

Such buildings automatically sustain the grading and encourage regular promotions." In the margin of his copy of the *Manual*, Flake wrote: "not so unless given special care."

On page 31 of his copy of the *Manual*, after a section about keeping the Sunday School graded, Flake added: "highly intellectual-religious-and social groups become exclusive, narrow, and small." He singled out groups that were defined by going into the details of a passage for the sake of gaining knowledge, viewed themselves as more spiritually mature than the other groups, or whose purpose was more about being with each other to the exclusion of those in the community who were not yet involved in any Bible study group. He knew those attitudes worked against reaching the community for Bible study. He had heard it and seen it before.

Flake identified other obstacles and excuses to be expected. On the two pages that contain his initial plan for reaching a community (Flake's Formula), right after his statements about everyone needing to study the Bible, he identified two excuses people gave for not giving his plan a try. He wrote: "We tried that" and "Won't work here."

Think about that for a moment. People may have tried some of the things Flake was proposing, but they had not tried all of it in the way he had proposed it. Second, how do you know it will not work until you try it? People say we live in a more complex era and are much more sophisticated today. Before we pat ourselves on the backs, we should list excuses given for not doing something in the church. Now take your list and see how many of those excuses can be categorized as either "tried that before" or "will not work here." You will discover our excuses have not changed or become more sophisticated!

On page 29 of his copy of the *Manual*, Flake identified more excuses and obstacles that could be expected. The comments are in response to Spilman's explanation for why Sunday Schools should be age-graded. Spilman stated that grading makes is easier for a School to reach and hold its consistency and grading makes it easier for a School to do effective teaching. Flake added a third reason, writing these words: "definitely fixes responsibility for each lost person in the community."

At the bottom of the page, Flake wrote a list of "difficulties to be met":

- *Do not understand what it means*
- *Not enough teachers*
- *Not enough room*
- *Pupils will leave Sunday School*
- *Many teachers desire to keep present pupils*

When he transferred his margin comments to the notes on the blank pages, he added quotation marks to the middle three difficulties, and reworded the first to "Supt.—Pastor and Teachers do not understand the advantages to be gained."

In Flake's 1922 book, the three items in quotation marks—not enough teachers, not sufficient room, and pupils will leave the Sunday School—were identified as "imagined difficulties."[30] These three things were recast as excuses given for not doing the hard work of relaunching and regrouping on an annual basis.

The real issues were pastors and teachers who didn't understand the advantages, and teachers who wanted their group to stay just the way it was.[31] As a group leader myself, I can understand why we covet our group members. We want people sitting in our class. We also want people who help spur the discussions forward as we gather for Bible study. This is one reason why, when a leader over one of the various groups—a Sunday school director, minister of education, or perhaps the pastor—asks teachers for names of potential leaders, we are tempted to share group members who are "less than the best"— those who are somewhat regular attenders but not the "A-players." Flake knew we might do that! In the 1922 book, Flake identified ongoing training for all people including pastors and keeping the purpose of reaching the community for Bible study as the means for addressing these two real difficulties.[32]

Flake knew what he was proposing would be met with some resistance. None of the opposition was new or surprising. The same should be expected today. We should expect the same excuses and similar resistance. Years may have passed, but we are still humans with the same insecurities, fears, and excuses.

One more factor stands out in Flake's notes that demands our attention. This factor overcomes all obstacles and is the backbone of his strategy for church growth. To neglect this factor would remove the teeth of the strategy and strip the power from the plan. That factor is *prayer*.

Prayer as the Driving Force

Most of us would say we believe in prayer. Most of us would classify our groups as being dedicated to prayer. We start the group time with prayer. We close the group time with prayer. We gather prayer requests to be shared with the group. We send messages so that our group members know we prayed for them.

Sometimes we get lost in the mechanics and move past the item that drives the mechanics in the first place. We see that when looking at Flake's Formula. We gather the names of people who are not in a Bible study group to enable us to make wise decisions for expanding the organization. It makes sense that we base the expansion of the organization on the names we collect, but a more significant reason exists for gathering names, and we find that in Flake's notes.

In his notes about the role ongoing Bible studies play in reaching a community, we find these words: "Every teacher should have a prayer list of all lost pupils and all who should belong in each class," and we also see the word "census." Let's look at this in two parts. First of all, the prayer list of unchurched and unaffiliated people.

Think about the prayer lists most of us carry or manage. Most are dominated by physical needs, ministry actions, and family problems. When we come together with other teachers and leaders, we usually share these needs with the group so that they can pray as well. Certainly, these are important, but we must ask ourselves if these requests carry eternal consequences. Do they impact the eternal destiny of the people for whom we are praying? That is the point with Flake's approach. We must focus on praying for the lost by name because their eternity depends upon it.

Here is the scenario Flake had in mind. A teacher carries a list of people he knows to be spiritually lost, and he is praying daily for each person listed by name. Every person in that teacher's class also has a list of people they know to be lost. The group members share their lists with the teacher so that he can join them in praying for all the lost people they personally know. These may be neighbors, family members, coworkers, people who do business with us, or people we greet every Tuesday morning on our walk. As a group, the teacher and his group members pray for this list of lost people every day. They ask God to soften the lost people's hearts, for opportunities for them to hear the gospel, and for God to use the members of the Bible study group in the process. Not only does one group pray this way, but every group prays this way. EVERY group for EVERY age.

When the teachers and leaders of all the groups come together for their regular training and planning times, one of the items on the agenda is the prayer lists of each group. Instead of sharing about surgeries, job changes, and other challenges being faced, the teachers share the names of the lost people for whom their groups are praying.

This is where the "census" part of this action comes into play. As these group prayer lists are shared, a larger "master list" of names is created. The pastor and other church leaders can then join each and every group in praying for these lost people by name. When new groups are started, this master prayer list serves as the starting point. When this happens, the church creates classes for people for whom many already have prayed at every level within the church's organizational structure.

Flake viewed ongoing Bible study groups (what he called Sunday School) as the greatest tool available for reaching a community for Christ. He believed lost, seekers, and unaffiliated persons all ought to be in a Bible study group. He wanted them there because he knew if they could just look at the Bible for themselves, they would find Christ. He also knew that this kind of work only happens through consistent prayer.

We are left to wonder what would happen if we took that approach in today's church. What if our prayer lists were dominated by the names of lost people we interacted with every week? What if we prayed for all those lost people by name every day?

So What?

Flake's notes and comments remind us that these leaders in the early 1900s faced many of the same challenges faced by church leaders today. They had a need to find and develop more workers. They had teachers who guarded their group members and fought the starting of new groups. They heard a variety of excuses today's leaders still hear: *people will leave if you start a new group, we don't have space, we don't have enough teachers, we tried that before,* and *it will not work here.*

But they believed people needed to study the Bible … in a group and as individuals … because everyone has spiritual needs that only God can meet. God's Word changes lives. Every believer ought to serve in some way in the local church. Local churches should intentionally seek to disciple everyone in their community. Creating more groups was critical for reaching communities with the gospel and for the future of local churches. Ongoing training was a must if they were going to succeed. These leaders saw a need and presented a strategic plan for meeting that need. That plan was based on a belief that God uses the Bible to change people's lives.

CHAPTER 3

Know Your Possibilities

David Apple

Notice People

When was the last time you asked Jesus to walk with you as you
go through your day? Sometimes, He'll help you notice people you
routinely see. He'll help you notice individuals as well as crowds you
may never have known as you journey from one place to another.
Walk with Jesus throughout your community. Whom do you think
He would point out to you? What kinds of people might He lead
you to notice? Would Jesus call attention to busy people? What
about those who are lonely? How about individuals whose friends
and family members have forgotten them? Perhaps He would point
out the successful people who no longer even acknowledge they need
Him. Jesus just might help you see people who are willing to be
engaged in Bible study, in ministry, or to be introduced to Him for
the first time. Might Jesus point out these future disciples, and more?

Imagine the Master asking questions like: "Have you noticed the
people where you live like I notice them? Have you seen the potential
that I see in them? Have you prayed for them like My Word has
taught you to do? Have you reached out to them like I modeled and
reached out to you?"

One of the significant principles highlighted by Arthur Flake was:
We must KNOW OUR POSSIBILITIES. The Master taught and
modeled this principle regarding His kingdom commission. We
must open our eyes to the individuals and people groups who are
part of the ministry field where God has placed us. We should be
compelled to pray for them, nurture and invite them, and be open to
divine appointments as God is at work in their lives and in ours. We
need to intentionally invite and minister to them through our Bible
study groups.

Discover and pray for people along your journey. Cultivate a list of the possible people and people groups who need to be nurtured, enrolled, invited, and discipled. Gather contact information on these individuals. These are people who can be described by one or more of the following:

- *Individuals experiencing crises, challenges, and life transitions.*
- *People looking for hope.*
- *People living in rebellion against God and needing a Savior.*
- *Individuals identifying as part of the church whether they attend or not.*
- *Individuals God identifies in Luke 15.*

Know the Possibilities Throughout God's Word

Celebrate some of many examples in Scripture that demonstrate how God sees the possibilities in people:

- **Matthew 9:36-38.** *Jesus saw the multitudes after He had interacted with a wide variety of individuals. He demonstrated compassion, an overflowing expression of God's grace.*
- **Deuteronomy 31:12-13.** *God instructed His people to gather persons of all ages as well as outsiders so they can hear and learn to fear the Lord, obey, and share what God's Word says.*
- **John 4:3-42.** *Jesus encountered the Samaritan woman who experienced a divine appointment; she became the first missionary to the Samaritans.*
- **Isaiah 61:1-3.** *People around us are poor, brokenhearted, and captive; and they mourn. Jesus read this Scripture to introduce His ministry. He shared strategies He would model and would teach us to pursue.*
- **Acts 9.** *Some people around us are like Saul/Paul. Believers in Christ thought of him as a terrorist, but God saw a potential missionary and gospel champion. We encounter people like Ananias and Barnabas (who were available to help Paul start on a journey of discipleship). We meet people like Peter, Aeneas, and Dorcas who experienced personal transformation by the Lord.*

We have remarkable opportunities to know and nurture people with the love and power of the gospel. We get to connect them to God's Word and Christian service, particularly by inviting them to be part of a Bible study group that expects new people each week. [33] Let's look at some of the opportunities we have to KNOW THE POSSIBILITIES through a Bible study group as well as a church.

Know your Members

Every church needs a list of its members. A person cannot join the church unless they acknowledge their sin, trust that Jesus died for them, and experience believer's baptism. Most churches acknowledge that on average, 40-60 percent of their members attend on a regular basis. That means many members are not participating in Bible study or ministry. [34] "Be sure that all of those attending your worship on a regular basis are assigned to a Sunday school class. They are more likely to attend if they are receiving ministry as well as invitations not only to Bible study but to fellowship opportunities as well." [35]

Every Bible study group also needs a current list of members. These are individuals who have accepted an invitation to be on the receiving end of prayer, Bible study, ministry, and fellowship. A person can join the Bible study group with or without trusting Jesus as Savior. A healthy group will acknowledge that an average of 40-60 percent of those enrolled attend on a regular basis. We want believers to be in Bible study; we also want non-believers to be enrolled and nurtured through a group. [36]

This raises questions for us to ponder:

- *Do we know and nurture relationships with absentee group members?*
- *Do we know and nurture relationships with guests who visit our Bible study group?*
- *Do we know and nurture relationships with people whom we would classify as regular attenders?*
- *Do we know and nurture relationships with people who are not involved in Bible study but might be a part of our group?*

- *Do we know and seek to build connections with members who are engaged in worship or other ministry opportunities but are not connected with a Bible study group?*

We must find opportunities for specific ministry, prayer, and Christian fellowship with the different kinds of people mentioned above. "Our ultimate objective is not merely for them to attend but for them to be on the receiving end as well as giving end of Christian discipleship." [37]

Your group will have attenders and absentees. A rule of thumb in group life is: the more members you have enrolled and are nurturing, the more people will typically participate in group Bible study. In many groups, 45-55 percent of a group's enrolled members will actually be in attendance. To put it another way, a group that averages 25 people on its ministry list will most likely have 12-13 people sitting in chairs and participating in the group's Bible study. We can and need to increase the number of individuals who agree to be enrolled in the ministry of a Bible study group. Individuals can be added to our ministry list (group roll) by merely agreeing to become part of the group; they do not need to earn specific attendance markers before becoming part of the group. We can value our absentee members by praying with them and looking for ministry opportunities rather than ignoring them or threatening to take them off our roll when their absences mount. The more people we know as part of our enrollment, the more opportunities we have to help them on the receiving end as well as the giving end of discipleship.

Know Possible Prospects

A prospect is someone not engaged in Bible study but with whom we should seek to nurture, pray for, and invite to a group. These can be believers not engaged in Bible study (they may attend worship only) but they also can include non-believers! A rule of thumb is: discover contact information and build relationships with at least as many prospects as we have members. [38] If we do not have an open group that targets a particular age or affinity group of the prospects, we have opportunity to start a group with that focus. Arthur Flake wrote, "Each teacher should have a prayer list both of the lost pupils in his class and of the lost who are prospects for his class …The habit of daily intercessory prayer will make over any Christian and any church, and cause streams of salvation to flow like rivers." [39]

Discover and nurture prospects throughout the year as you participate in ministry, fellowship, evangelism, and discipleship experiences. We want to make sure every believer is invited and given opportunity to be on the receiving end and the giving end of growing as a follower of Christ! We will find opportunities when we intentionally pray for and connect with unsaved persons. Always look for persons who are not connected to a Bible study group; look for those who do not have a saving faith in Jesus Christ. To create a list of prospects, consider implementing any of the following ideas:

- *"Who do you know?" cards. Many churches occasionally distribute index cards on which persons are invited to write the name and contact information of a person(s) they know who is not involved in Bible study and/or has no relationship with the Lord. The information from cards like these can help believers pray for and pursue ministry opportunities for these persons.*

- *Worship attenders or guests; church members not enrolled in Bible study.* [40]

- *Persons who participate in ministry or fellowship opportunities.*

- *FRANs—Friends, Relatives, Associates, and Neighbors.*

- *Persons discovered through Religious Census. Gather names, ages, and contact information of all within the household. Ask residents about church involvement; ask for permission to enroll them in Bible study. Ask for opportunities to pray for residents.*

- *"Ten most wanted." Identify a specific list of ten individuals you most urgently want to participate in Bible study or you want to know Jesus as Savior. Intentionally pray for, build relationship with, invite, and minister to persons on your list. Display your list on a prominent place in your home or office as a reminder to pray for and look for divine appointments with these persons.*

- *Identify people in specific life stages. Life stages include preschoolers, children, and students; newly or nearly weds; parents of preschoolers, kid, and students; single/again adults; empty-nesters; recently grieved.*

- *Identify persons who relate to an affinity group. These include individuals who have something in common like military personnel and families, parents or an age range, or those who speak English as a second language. You may discover persons who have recently moved, changed jobs, or other transition or defining group. Your lists will continue to grow as you become more aware of the people Jesus points out to you.*

- *The church where I serve has placed the name of every member (if they regularly attend or not) on a yellow slip of paper and attached each one to a large wooden cross. We also place names of people we know from our community who are not engaged in a Bible study group and/or have no relationship through faith in our Lord on orange slips of paper. This has become a tangible way of our literally taking people to the cross. Thus, we are reminded to pray for and seek opportunities to minister to each of these individuals.*

Know your Leadership Possibilities

You also get to open your eyes to and nurture individuals who are or could be serving in a ministry. As you support current and previous workers, know that God is always raising up individuals to serve; pray for, nurture, and help encourage these persons. I often fail to notice and know people who are like Saul of Tarsus on whom God had His hand. I was leading evangelism training in a rough, major U.S. city neighborhood. It was a dangerous place. However, many people from the area came to receive training, visited people in that community, and returned to report. After the event concluded, I was intrigued with a mature lady who had been there to participate and provided help cleaning up. I was genuinely concerned about her leaving by herself. I remember asking her, "Why are you doing this knowing you live in such a dangerous community?" She said, "We had this kind of training several years ago, and the person who led the training said something that changed my life. He said we were going out to 'look for the next Billy Graham. Right now,' he said, 'Billy is an eight year old who has never known his father; his mom is a drug addict and is not at all supportive. Matter of fact, Billy has never been to this or any church. Our job is to find Billy. God has something very special to do through Billy, but he doesn't know it!'"

Opportunities for Finding the Next Billy

Where do we go to find that child for whom God has a special place? Here are some ideas to get you started.

On-Campus Special Events

- *Vacation Bible School*

- *Attenders at special events held at the church. The small, rural church where I serve has events like Back to School parties for kids and their parents, Fall Festival/"Trunk or Treat," and Easter Egg Hunt where we intentionally invite neighbors to come on our property. Your church or group may help sponsor other events where you invite and can start nurturing individuals who come to you.*

Community-centered Events

- *Identify short term ministry projects to individuals, neighborhoods and through agencies in your community. A group can adopt a family or group of families during special seasons. A group can adopt students or teachers in a local school, first responders, or other local agencies where members seek to assist and build relationships with others. A group or church can collect food or clothing and provide it for individuals in your community. Gather contact information about these persons, and intentionally pray for and invite them.*

- *Sponsor neighborhood or block parties.*

- *Routinely make visits in homes or businesses of persons you discover; visit hospitals, health care facilities, and home bound individuals. Intentionally connect with persons on their turf.*

- *Show up at recreation areas where parents are with their kids; support the kids as you build relationships with parents and grandparents.*

People with Common Interests or Life Stages

- *Look for people who speak your language or have some of your same interests or background. Look for people who have similar job assignments, live in the same neighborhood including single family or multi-family dwellings, or have similar hobbies or leisure preferences.*

- *My wife and I are parents of two adult children. We tend to relate to others who are parents. We also have three young grandchildren; all live a long distance from us. Our youngest grandson lives with the effects of spinal meningitis and strokes he contracted at age three months. We thus identify with individuals living with special health and developmental needs. We also have a rapport with people who are in health care and therapy professions.*

- *Both my wife and I have family members with Alzheimer's disease. We are learning a new level of sensitivity and empathy with people who deal with various health challenges. We all have opportunity to nurture relationships with and pray specifically for individuals and families because we have commonalities.*

People Who Are Different From You

- *Look for people who have differences such as age, life stage, economic level, skin color, religion, or language. Differences can help us notice divine appointments.*

- *During the past decade I have been volunteering in a maximum security prison and have been assigned to work with inmates and staff on death row. These men are different from me in many ways, but the Lord has helped me see ways He works in this and other "different" situations. He orchestrates our lives to discover individuals for whom He died.*

- *I have been able to travel and teach recently in several countries in East Asia. I have encountered people of all ages who do not speak my language. Their background, culture, history, and religion (if any) are very different from mine. Yet, as I returned to my country I have noticed more people who have different language, culture, heritage, and religion from mine. As we walk with Jesus, He orchestrates our lives to discover people in whose lives He is at work.*

Grow to Know the Lord

The living Lord is in charge of His church and of all creation. He loves all people because He created them in His image. He became the sacrifice to restore each one to Himself. He has placed us in specific parts of His field for us to plant, cultivate, and be part of the harvest. He places individuals and people groups as divine appointments where He chooses. He has the right to move others and us around as part of His plans. The Lord is the One who produces fruit, and we cannot take credit for what only He can do. He speaks through His Holy Spirit and His Word, and He allows us to join Him at work. He wants us to experience the joy of growing in grace and helping disciple others. He wants us to walk with Him. He wants us to know Him.

Kevin is someone who is dynamically in love with Jesus. He is a prayer warrior and a student of God's Word. He now loves people, and he looks for opportunities to nurture others in a life transforming relationship with the Lord who has dramatically transformed him. Kevin recently shared that he gets "to be a missionary." Although I was enthusiastic about his confidence in the Lord, I admittedly was hesitant to endorse his assignment. He then started pointing around where we were standing. (Did I mention that Kevin is an inmate on death row and was pointing at all the cells of residents in the "pod" where he is housed?) He said, "I know and get to pray for all these men every day; I AM a missionary."

I responded, "Kevin, from now on, I am going to treat you like you're a missionary." Since then, I have grown to know, build relationships with, and pray for many other men in the complex where Kevin resides. These men likely will never attend our churches, but God is working whether we open our eyes or not to see Him at work.

Let prayer be a significant part of your ministry to reach people. Realize we know and will discover many people in our ministry field. Gather information and connect them to your church, your group, and to each other. You and your group may be an answer to prayer for some of the people we will get to know. Let's continue letting Jesus walk with us as He connects us with people He wants us to KNOW.

CHAPTER 4

Enlarge the Organization

Bruce Raley

As Arthur Flake spelled out his "formula" to guide a Sunday School toward fulfilling its purpose, it began with knowing the possibilities. The next step, enlarging the organization, is crucial, yet it is often overlooked in the administration of Sunday School. If this second step is not embraced, however, the formula falls apart. Flake knew that "enlarging the organization" was not optional, but critical if a church is to have a growing, thriving Sunday School.

In his book, *Building a Standard Sunday School,* Flake emphasized, *"There will be no use to go on with the same old organization hoping to increase the size of Sunday School permanently."*[41] In Flake's era, enlarging the organization primarily meant starting new groups. Expanding the number of groups was necessary if a Sunday School was going to grow, teach, and serve. More people required more groups. This principle is still true. But this practice of expansion can be broadened in today's culture. Not only are new groups needed, but many communities need churches to offer new times and perhaps even additional days for Sunday School beyond Sunday morning, to reach people whose jobs require them to work on Sundays.

The Biblical Concept of Enlarging the Organization

The concept of additional groups (enlarging the organization) is not only practical, but even more important, it's biblical. Second Kings 4:1-7 tells us about a miracle involving a widow and her sons. Her late husband had been a man who feared the Lord and was called "one ... of the sons of the prophets (v. 1)." After her husband died, the widow and her two children were alone, with no one to care for them. They had very few resources. A creditor to whom the family owed money soon would enslave her children to fulfill the debt.

The prophet Elisha asked the woman what she had left. She told him she only had a single jar of oil. Elisha instructed her to borrow empty containers from her neighbors; not just a few, but as many as she could gather. She then was to pour the oil from her jar into the borrowed containers to fill them. Her sons kept bringing the containers and she kept pouring the oil. Here God stepped in. Her original container of oil continued to fill all of the borrowed containers, one after the other. The oil stopped when all the containers were full and no more empty ones were left to fill.

It's important for churches and church leaders to understand some principles from this passage. Let's begin by understanding that God has a mission for every church. That mission is to fulfill the Great Commission, which tells the church to "go and make disciples." God wants every church to reach people with the gospel and to see those people mature in Christ.

The Bible tells us that evangelism and discipleship occurs best in the context of relationships. Within the ministry of the church, relationships develop best in smaller groups. The larger the group, the less likely deeper relationships will develop. Smaller groups simply provide greater opportunity for people to know and care for one another, openly converse and confide in each other, work together on projects and missions, and share life together. All of these actions develop relationships that grow and deepen. For churches to continue to reach more people, we must create new groups (containers). Let's learn from the story of the widow, her miracle, and its implication for the church and Sunday School today.

1. Increase the number of containers (v. 3). Elisha did not ask the widow to find one or two more containers, but to borrow empty containers from everyone. She was to go to all her neighbors, friends, and relatives to ask for empty containers. In fact, Elisha told her specifically, "Do not get just a few." If empty containers (new groups) are needed in order to include more people in our churches, we cannot focus on gathering just one or two. We should not set our goals and sights on "just a few," but on many. In other words, we should strive to launch many new groups every year, expecting all of those groups to reach new people.

2. God fills the containers (vv. 5-6). Elisha did not bring in oil to fill the containers. God miraculously filled the empty containers. The widow and her sons worked to gather the containers. She obeyed the prophet by pouring her oil into the empty containers. But it was God that filled them. He took the little oil she already had and multiplied it many times over.

Launching new groups takes hard work. We must enlist and train leaders. We determine a suitable meeting place. We choose the content of study (curriculum). We are to obey the Lord in fulfilling the Great Commission by seeking and inviting people. But with all of those efforts on our part, it is up to God to "fill the containers." He is the one who causes His church to grow.

First Corinthians 12:18 tells us that God places people into the body as He sees fit. *"But as it is, God has arranged each one of the parts in the body just as he wanted."*

3. Involve others (v. 3). The prophet did not do all the work. Many people were involved. The widow. Her sons. Their neighbors. All of these had a part in this miracle. The launch of new groups requires the involvement of many. A pastor, a minister of education, or a Sunday School leader alone can only do so much. But when many are involved, the possibilities are much greater. For example, if the woman had involved more neighbors ... borrowed more empty containers ... she ultimately would have had more oil. The secret to success is involving people. This requires "all hands on deck."

4. Containers can only hold so much (v. 4). Elisha instructed the widow to fill the containers and then set them aside when they were full. While the original container held a seemingly endless supply of oil, the additional containers would only hold so much. When they were full, they were full—then it was time to move to a new container and continue the filling. Groups come in all sizes, just like the containers. Some groups are large. Some are really small. In fact, a group can even be composed of only two people. There is no perfect size group. However, every group has a "full" limit. While the numbers of people may vary, every group maximizes its effectiveness at some point. Many factors are involved in determining when a group is full. Some of these factors are obvious, such as the size of the meeting location. It is impossible, for example, to get twenty people in a space that can only hold ten! But some are more subjective, such as the maximum number that allows for a group to engage in conversation. Important also is the number of people the group can adequately serve. Another sign that a group may be maxing out is the people's ability to know everyone's names and information about their lives. Here's reality: when a group reaches that maximum number it can care for and relate to, it cannot continue to grow. The container is full.

5. A catalyst is needed (v. 3). The widow poured the oil. The Lord miraculously filled the containers. But the Lord used the prophet to initiate it all. Very few—VERY few groups—just spring up of their own volition. New groups are not like tree sprigs that just pop up out of roots. New groups are started with intentionality. And we need a person—a catalyst—for that initiation. Because God places people into the body of the church as He sees fit, He has a place where He wants them. This is a place where they will be loved, cared for, challenged to grow, and asked to serve. Therefore, God will place on the hearts of church leaders the need for new groups. He will place a burden for certain types of groups on the hearts of the church's leaders so that everyone has a place to study the Bible. All leaders and teachers should be prayerful, expectant, and open to the Lord's voice in the creation of new groups.

6. When there are no more empty containers, the oil will stop flowing (v. 6). The sons kept on bringing empty containers to their mother. She kept pouring from her original oil container. But when the last container was filled, the oil stopped flowing. God stopped sending more oil for the widow and her sons. Why would church leaders today think God will send more people when there is no place for them in a group (the "container")? If a group is full, why would the Lord add more to that group? If we desire to fulfill the Great Commission, we must always provide new containers that can hold more. Not just one or two, but many … expecting the Lord to fill those containers with people who need Him and His Word.

Two Great Goals in Enlarging the Organization

The Word of God says, "We proclaim him, warning and teaching everyone with all wisdom, so that we may present everyone mature in Christ" (Colossians 1:28). Pastors and church leaders desperately desire to see great goals realized in their churches. We want to see more people being reached for Christ, and more people becoming mature in Christ. Arthur Flake knew the creation of new Bible study groups had proved to be a great vehicle to accomplish those objectives.

If you have walked down a railroad track, you have probably observed an optical illusion. When looking down the track into the distance, it appears that the two rails get closer and closer until they finally merge together. But we know they don't merge and never will. Standard railroad tracks are always four feet, eight and a half inches apart. [42] Considering the two great goals of people being reached for Christ and people being matured in Christ, it appears these two goals should merge together. But in reality, these two seldom merge.

We can find many examples of churches that have focused on only one of those goals, even to the detriment of the other. The 1970's and 80's are sometimes labeled the "church growth movement" years. Churches focused heavily on "reaching people for Christ." But by the 90's, many church leaders declared their congregations "a mile wide, but only an inch deep." They felt that spiritual growth had not occurred among the people they had reached with the gospel.

In these later years, spiritual maturation has become the focus. While leaders have used various names for these efforts, such as spiritual development, spiritual growth, discipleship, and so forth, the goal is for people to grow deeper in their faith. However, during this same time period, church attendance and participation have declined. The reality is that both are essential. A church should strive both to reach people for Christ and help them to grow spiritually once they accept Christ.

Using the railroad track as an analogy, the two primary goals are the tracks: reaching people for Christ and maturing people in Christ. They run parallel to one another. Ministries and strategies are necessary to see both occur. A common element, however, binds the two together and helps in accomplishing both goals. That element is enlarging the organization with new groups.

Realities of Enlarging the Organization

1. Discipleship takes place best in the context of relationships (groups). The ultimate goal of every Bible study group is to make disciples. A disciple is one who is being transformed into Christlikeness so that he or she thinks and acts like Christ. More groups allow for more and deeper relationships.

2. The Word of God is the focal point of groups. Relationships within a group are crucial. Organization for ministry is needed. A vision for the future provides guidance. But the foundation of a new group must be upon the study and discussion of God's Word. That is what makes the group's life transformational. Learning and living the gospel must have priority in all new groups. Flake understood the necessity of the Bible being the central point of a Sunday School group. "It has been suggested that the Bible is a living book on life— to be applied to life today. This should be a constant emphasis. Our Bible is not just the sacred literature of a broken and despised people; it is the living Word of God for every human being alive today. It has in it the medicine for every sickness, the payment for every debt, the answer to every heart-searching query, and the way of life for every lost soul who is willing to follow its teaching to the foot of Calvary's cross." [43]

3. Groups are needed at times other than just Sunday morning. The reality of today's culture is that many people cannot attend a group on Sunday morning even if they wanted to do so. Hundreds, even thousands, of people work in every community every Sunday. Hospitals, retail businesses, nursing homes, public service agencies and many more are open and working on Sundays. An April 2017 *Forbes* article cited a survey of 1,000 Americans that found around 70 percent of employees worked at least one weekend a month, and 63 percent said their boss expected them to work on Saturday and Sunday. [44]

Do we just ignore this reality and pretend that every person could come on Sundays if they really wanted to do so? Or, do we acknowledge reality and enlarge the organization by developing additional Bible study groups that meet at times during the week?

4. Groups are created pro-actively. Very few groups start organically. A perceived need often precipitates the creation of a new group or class. Take a look at the list below from the book *Extreme Sunday School Challenge* and think about your church. Is there an opportunity for a new group to reach some of these people?

- *Church members not involved in a group*
- *People who live in apartments and/or condominiums*
- *People in the workplace (hospitals, offices, etc.)*
- *People who live in your area seasonally ("snowbirds," campers, migrant workers)*
- *Parents whose children are in childcare centers*
- *Business executives or other work affinity groups*
- *Parents of preschoolers, children, youth, college students*
- *Empty nesters*
- *People with hobbies and special interests (motorcyclists, hunters, quilters, golfers, RVer's, etc.)*
- *Young couples who are newlywed or nearlywed*
- *New members to church*
- *People who might attend a weekday home group*
- *People who cannot attend Sunday morning, but can attend Wednesday or Sunday nights*
- *People who speak other languages (Internationals)*
- *People who need a recovery group*
- *Adults involved in the church's choir or worship team*
- *People who live in retirement homes or retirement villages*
- *People who have children with special needs*[45]

The "How-to" of Enlarging the Organization

Arthur Flake understood one of the most important actions a Sunday School could take is to start new groups. New groups reach new people, develop new leaders, make more disciples, and allow more people to exercise their spiritual gifts leading to greater spiritual maturity. New groups grow faster and tend to be more evangelistic than existing groups.

Churches that regularly start new groups in addition to the ones they already have almost always experience growth. Any church, regardless of its size, location, or ethnicity, can start new groups. Starting new groups requires a catalyst. Perhaps you are that catalyst. Do you have a passion for reaching new people, and are you willing to do the work it takes to make it happen? Here are steps to start a new group:

- **Identify the target for the group.** *Who is the new group intended to reach? Young Adults? Single Parents? Students? Children? Preschoolers? Parents with preschoolers? What segment of your congregation or community does not "fit" with existing small groups? Is there an age span that is too wide? Who attends worship but does not have a group that is designed for them?*

- **Select curriculum that the group will study.** *Curriculum provides doctrinal accountability for the teacher, as well as saving him or her time in preparation. Curriculum also gives group members a resource they can study between group meetings.*

- **Enlist people to help start the new group.** *Enlist people from other classes that fit the target audience of the new group. It's easier to start a group with a few friends who are willing to come together and provide energy and synergy to the new work. Start with at least three people who will serve as the core of the new group—the Bible study leader, someone responsible for reaching new people, and someone responsible for helping the new group engage in serving others.*

- **Develop a list of prospects for the new group.** *Develop a list with contact information of potential members for the new group. Make contact with these prospects, inviting them to participate in this new group.*

- **Select the starting date.** *Choose a date to start the new group. New groups can start at any time but most churches have discovered that new groups launch better in high growth times such as fall and at the beginning of a new year.*

- **Choose a time and location or room where the group will meet.**

- **Train the core team.** *Share your expectations for the new group. Let the leaders know you expect them to attend training opportunities you provide throughout the year. Help the group set goals for the number and frequency of fellowships and ministry projects they'll undertake each quarter. And be sure to talk about your expectations that the group will grow and ultimately "franchise" itself by starting a new group of its own.*

- **Focus on relationships early in the process.** *Plan and conduct a fellowship or interest party. Many people interested in a new group are looking to make new friends. Offer a fellowship before the start of the new group and invite as many potential participants as possible. Share about the new group and invite prospective group members to attend.*

- **Start.** *Make sure everything is ready. Arrive early and verify the room/space is ready to go. Be prepared to teach and lead the best lesson you possibly can. Allow time for fellowship and prayer.*

- **Evaluate, encourage, and celebrate.** *Evaluate the process, encourage your group, and celebrate as new people join. Follow up frequently with guests and work to build relationships with people. Encourage the group to plan fellowships and ministry projects.*

CHAPTER 5

Enlist and Train Workers

Steve Parr

Flake had a Driver

Have you ever observed that two churches ministering in the same community can have drastically different results with regard to their small group strategies? Both churches serve people with equivalent demographics, experience comparable financial support, and have similar pastors and facilities, yet one congregation struggles while the other congregation thrives. Why is that? You can likely identify several factors, but Arthur Flake wisely uncovered and taught a key element that has proven both biblically and quantifiably to make a difference in the likelihood that Sunday School, or similar ministries with a different name, can thrive. Flake understood the importance of a key element of Sunday school growth. It was so essential that he included it in his formula.

Why is it that group leaders in one church cooperate with church staff, while in another church they choose to operate much more independently? Why are the leaders in one church flexible about the allocation of Bible study spaces, but in another church they are overly protective? Why do teachers embrace outreach efforts in one church but ignore them in the other church? Why do teachers lead effective Bible studies with kids in one church but do little more than babysit in another? The answer to all of these questions is the same: *the churches that enlist properly and provide training for leaders clearly have stronger ministries led by more effective leaders.*

Enlisting leaders is critical, but if they are not trained they may struggle to be effective. Occasionally you will be blessed with an exceptional leader who is gifted and thrives with little external motivation and training. Flake understood that this was not the norm. Group leaders tend to do what they are trained to do.

Training is the driver that results in good teaching, good leadership, good administration, and effective Bible study groups.

Ongoing training has been proven to be a major determining factor in whether or not a church's Bible study ministry grows. A study of the fastest growing small groups in the state of Georgia revealed that the most common factor among growing churches was that they provided ongoing training for their leaders. The research revealed that congregations that provided at least four training sessions per year gained more than 13 percent in attendance during a four-year time span, while those that provided no training declined by an average of 2 percent during the same period of time. Training undoubtedly has the greatest influence on the growth of Bible study groups and is also a tremendous factor on whether or not you personally grow in your skills as a leader and a teacher.

What is meant by "training" in this context? Training is a systematic approach for conveying necessary skills to leaders that permit them to effectively carry out the ministry to which God has called them. Sadly, many churches enlist Bible study leaders, assign them a room and a group, provide them with some form of Bible study materials, and send them to do the work of ministry without ever providing any ongoing training. I never received any instruction on conducting outreach, enlisting leaders, ministering to absentees, creating new groups, or interpreting Scripture while I studied for my bachelor's degree in education; I had to learn those things "on the job." How much better would it have been if a church had trained me in those areas so that I could have been even more effective as a Bible study leader? I have assisted churches as a part of my ministry for almost thirty-five years, and I am still learning new things. Effective leaders are life-long learners. The reason that Bible teaching ministries in churches struggle is that they have wonderful people enlisted to serve who have not been equipped to do the work.

Pastors of today's churches have a biblical mandate to equip those who minister in and through the church. Paul reminded believers in Ephesians 4:11-12 that: "… *he himself gave some to be apostles, some prophets, some evangelists, some pastors and teachers, equipping the saints for the work of ministry, to build up the body of Christ.*" Equipping the members of the body to serve effectively is not a suggestion. It is imperative to equip those who lead preschoolers, children, students, and adults in Bible study and small groups. Vibrant churches find a way to equip their leaders. I often hear pastors and staff make excuses for why they cannot get their leaders involved in training. I know that it can be done, not only from personal experience but also from observing so many churches that make training a priority.

Paul often reminded Timothy of the importance of sharpening his skills. In 2 Timothy 1:6, Paul instructed Timothy to "rekindle the gift of God which is in you." In the second chapter he spoke of teaching skills when he said, "Be diligent to present yourself to God as one approved, a worker who doesn't need to be ashamed, correctly teaching the word of truth. Avoid irreverent and empty speech, since those who engage in it will produce even more godlessness (2 Tim 2:15-16)." Paul continues this theme in the third chapter by reminding Timothy that, "All Scripture is inspired by God, and is profitable for teaching, for rebuking, for correcting, for training in righteousness, so that the man of God may be complete, equipped for every good work (2 Tim 3:16-17)."

Being "equipped for every good work" is the aim of combining spiritual growth and development of skills. Skills are learned, often as the result of instruction provided by godly leaders. Later in chapter 4, Paul challenged Timothy with the words, "Exercise self-control in everything, endure hardship, do the work of an evangelist, fulfill your ministry (2 Tim 4:5)." This important work in ministry may or may not have been a spiritual gifting or a natural skill that Timothy possessed, but either way, he had to do the work and he had to share the gospel to fulfill his ministry calling. If Timothy did not possess the spiritual gifting, he certainly could have learned and improved upon his ability to share the gospel—all Christians are called to share their faith. If he did possess the gift of evangelism, that gift still could be strengthened through practice and other means. Timothy had a responsibility to develop his skills as a minister, as well as to grow in his relationship with God.

Our spiritual growth can lead to an enhancement of skills and gifts that we possess. As we find ourselves making strides and growing increasingly competent for ministry, it will fuel our passion to serve. Every ministry involves responsibilities that may or may not be addressed directly in Scripture. Maximizing our potential as Bible study leaders will require that we take advantage of opportunities to develop leadership skills. That begins by committing to participate in any and all equipping and training opportunities provided by the pastor and staff. Even if a church's leaders do not intentionally provide ongoing training for the church's volunteers, it does not absolve those lay leaders of the responsibility to "rekindle" the spiritual gifts God has placed in them.

Ed Stetzer and Mike Dodson conducted a study of over 300 churches that made a turnaround after experiencing many years of decline. Reprioritizing their leadership training was a common factor in the ability of those churches to reverse their decline. Surveys indicate the importance of a small group structure in connecting people to the life of the church and providing a place of service for church members. Those churches also noted an increased emphasis on building community and an expansion of the number of groups offered. To support these new groups, teacher training became a priority. One comeback leader indicated that an increased emphasis in Sunday School and increased teacher training were important factors in their comeback experience. The training gave teachers a clear set of priorities and showed them how to treat Sunday School classes or small groups. [46]

Evaluate Your Training

A lack of commitment on the part of lay leaders can be frustrating. However, we can begin the process of reversing that trend by evaluating our current systems. Are we providing training? Is the training worthy of the time our leaders are asked to invest? Consider where we are and how we can improve in the following areas:

1. Look at the schedule. Can we find a better time or a better way to deliver training to our leaders?

2. Look at the content. Are we genuinely helping our leaders develop their skills?

3. Look at the format. Are we providing inspiration as well as instruction?

4. Look at the delivery. Are we growing in our presentation skills?

5. Look at the priority. Are other activities or priorities competing with the training? Is it an expectation of our leaders?

6. Look at the logistics. Are we providing childcare for parents that are expected to participate?

7. Look at the promotion. Do our leaders know the subject matter in advance, and is it compelling?

Evaluation is painful because we may begin to realize the lack of commitment or skill of our leaders is directly correlated to the quality of our training or the lack thereof. The good news is that it does not require a large amount of financial resources to make a significant improvement. To improve the quality of our leadership will, however, require significant investment from a key leader. Improving the quality of ongoing training will not resolve the problems entirely, but it can positively affect the degree of participation.

Survey Our Current Leaders

We can conduct much of the evaluation ourselves, and we will likely know the answers to most of the questions we will ask—but ask anyway, just to be sure we have a good pulse on the hearts and minds of our people. Seek to discover the needs of the volunteers, and what adjustments might strengthen their commitment to participate in training. A survey can take the form of personal interviews with a few key leaders, a focus group that gathers for discussion and planning, or a written survey completed by every leader. The key is to hear the heart of our leaders and to respond to their needs. Ask about timing, topics, quality, standards, options, and ideas for improvement. Remember this key point when surveying leaders: the question is not whether training should be provided but how and when to provide training that enhances the skills of every leader and compels them to want to participate. A survey will be of no value without a commitment to implement. Determine which ideas are applicable and map out a plan to incorporate the best ideas.

Train the Trainable

We must not base our success in training on the number of participants that show up, but rather on our responsibility to provide it. Arthur Flake did not randomly include training in his formula to inflate the process. He knew the impact good training could bring to a church's lay leaders. My own leadership testimony reflects my strategic decision to begin increasing an emphasis on enlisting new leaders throughout the year and investing times of training in them.

While all leaders should be expected to participate in equipping opportunities, we have a responsibility biblically to provide those opportunities whether a large or small percentage choose to participate. While Ephesians 4:11-12 (equipping of the saints) is the responsibility of pastors, it is clear that the members are expected to participate in the training that the pastor provides. While we should equip no matter how many leaders participate, we should do all we can to maximize the involvement of our leaders.

What if only a few leaders participate in training? What if we only get a handful of leaders to go to a training experience at our church, or perhaps at an off-site training provided by denominational agencies, parachurch organizations, or other churches? Provide the training. Train the trainable and have a great time doing it even if the numbers are small. Perhaps their experience will have a positive effect not only on their ministry but also on other leaders as they hear about the experiences of those who participate.

A Systematic Plan

When is the next training session scheduled for our leaders? If we don't know the answer to that question, then our leaders don't know either, and they will not see training as a priority. Each year the pastor and key leaders should develop a 12-month training plan for group leaders. Imagine giving these volunteers a 12-month plan well in advance of the first training event. What will that accomplish? First, we will communicate the importance and the priority of training by working and planning in advance. Second, we will minimize conflicts by getting dates on the church calendar as well as on the calendars of the volunteers. Third, we will maximize the promotion, preparation, and quality of the experience, resulting in increased participation.

Should we meet weekly, monthly, or quarterly? We should start where we are, but be careful not to overwhelm leaders with initial plans. We might begin with a few gatherings this year and increase the frequency based on our church's unique culture. Here are several options that we can mix and match to create a customizable plan to equip our leaders, and I will follow with how to build in accountability.

1. The On-Site Launch: Plan a two- to three-hour orientation to kick off the new cycle of groups. Invite outside leaders, if possible, to come to your church and pour into your church's leaders so that they can hear from other credible sources. Review policies, procedures, standards, and training plans.

2. The Off-Site Conference: Take a group of leaders to a training conference in your state or region. Many churches, parachurch organizations, and state denominations provide a variety of conferences that can benefit your church's leaders. Don't base commitment to participate on the size of the group that is willing to attend. Making a difference in the lives and abilities of even a few leaders can make a huge difference in your groups and your church.

3. The Banquet: Provide an appreciation banquet for our church's leaders and integrate a speaker or training to enhance the opportunity. The banquet does not have to be formal but it should be well prepared and inspirational.

4. The Breakfast/Lunch Option: Provide training at both breakfast and lunch on a given Sunday. Allow leaders to attend one or the other. Yes. That means that we do it twice in one day but it gives options to our leaders. When promoting the events, do not ask "if they are attending" but "which of the two" they plan to attend.

5. The Standard: Plan quarterly, bi-monthly, or monthly training sessions for the volunteers.

6. The Proxy: Purchase a book for all leaders, ask them to read it, and organize discussion groups to follow up.

7. The $^{24}\!/_7$ option: Identify online resources such as podcasts, videos, audio books, sermons, or other sources available to leaders and get the proper links to each person with an expectation of participation and follow up. Each person can view or listen on his or her own schedule.

8. The Quick Pitch: Record a brief five- to ten-minute leadership lesson using a source such as "Screencast-o-matic" and email it to the leaders each week (or every other week). I call this "training in drips" and recently got great response from this approach in a church where I served.

9. The Marathon: Plan a full evening of training from dinner until late at night on a Friday evening. Make it fun and inspirational. The best example I have seen of this strategy was at First Baptist of Houston, Texas at an event they call "Midnight Madness." They literally provide several hours of training leading up to midnight.

10. The Retreat: Get away with our leaders for an overnight retreat at a conference center or hotel. We can also have a "stay at home retreat" but we will have people coming and going if we are near everyone's home.

This list of ideas is certainly not exhaustive. The key is to provide several opportunities and several hours of training throughout the year. Develop a plan, promote it to all leaders, and implement with excellence. We should build in accountability. Here are three ways:

1. Through Expectation: Communicate to all leaders the expectation that everyone will participate in "x" number of hours of training in the coming twelve months. Do not overwhelm the leaders with expectations that are too high or fail to stretch them by expecting too little. If we are just starting out we will do well to expect eight to ten hours.

2. Through Covenant: This higher level of accountability invites leaders to commit to a minimum number of hours of training in the course of a year. We agree with the leader on the number of hours expected, the opportunities that are offered, and a signed commitment to accomplish the training both of us have agreed to do. Be cautious by introducing covenants slowly and wisely. The covenant should initially be an invitation, but as we work with leaders over the course of several years it may become an expectation.

3. Through Acknowledgement: Be sure to acknowledge and affirm those leaders who participate and who meet the benchmarks set forth in expectations or covenants. Show appreciation and recognition along the way, but highlight accomplishments on an annual basis. Recognition can be public and tangible, but it should always be personal.

Remember that those who lead the groups in our churches are volunteers. They are not looking for financial reimbursement, but the currency of appreciation will go a long way toward inspiring each person to participate in the training that we suggest or provide.

Conclusion

Enlist and train the leaders. Why did Flake include this in his formula? Is it not easier to simply enlist leaders and assign them a group? The problem of enlisting without training is two-fold. First, we will struggle with enlistment if we do not provide training. Trained leaders will do much of the enlistment for us over time because they will be much more effective in recruiting new leaders. The ultimate task of any leader is to enlist and develop more leaders. Second, untrained leaders will only do what they know to do and will often do less. We will occasionally be blessed with a natural born leader who will lead a dynamic group. What about the rest of our volunteers? What about people who are untrained, busy, stretched, and have no formal education for leading groups? Even the professional educators in our churches received no academic training in outreach, group administration, use of space, enlistment, theology, and dozens of other issues that can make a Bible study leader much more effective. Everyone, and I mean *everyone*, needs training! Flake's Formula is a proven strategy, and equipping is at the core of his formula. More important is the biblical mandate to equip all generations. What is your plan?

CHAPTER 6

Provide Space and Resources

Alan Raughton

A church that is serious about reaching, teaching, and serving through the Sunday School or other ongoing Bible study groups knows the importance of providing appropriate space and resources to accomplish this work. Arthur Flake understood the importance of adequate space. "There is no such thing as building a Sunday school great in numbers in small, cramped quarters. Neither can a Sunday school of the highest efficiency be operated without proper equipment. While good equipment does not necessarily guarantee an efficient Sunday school, at the same time, it is necessary if a Sunday school is to do the best quality of work."[47] The same holds true today.

Our churches must consider the right amount of space as well as the type of space each age group needs. Other considerations are the location of the rooms based on the age group or mobility of the group assigned to use the space. All rooms should be neat, clean, and include the right type and size of equipment and resources appropriate for the age group occupying the space.

Where to Start

Flake called for the adjusting of present space as the starting point.[48] Church facilities with education space represent the church's largest investment. It is a valuable asset in making disciples, so we should maximize how the space is utilized. Determine the square footage of each classroom and potential classroom (some churches have turned valuable classroom space into large storage rooms). Clean out the clutter and start new groups in those rooms!

Create a document listing every room with the room number, the square footage of the room (measure the length and the width of each room; multiply the two figures to determine the total square footage of the room), the age group assigned to the room, the maximum number of people the room will hold based on the age group using the room, and how many people it will hold if it is 80 percent full. Why calculate 80 percent capacity of the room? Experience has shown that a classroom is functionally full at 80 percent of its capacity and growth will slow down; in some cases, attendance drops if people feel too crowded. [49] A chart is provided in the appendix with recommended square footage based on age groups. (See Appendix for Chart: Meeting Space Recommendations, p. 106.)

As we move through our building, we may find rooms that are not in use. Look for vacant rooms, large closets or other places (such as choir rooms not in use) where a potential class could meet. If the church owns residences or other buildings nearby, include these as possible Sunday School meeting spaces as well.

Beware of Expensive "Space Killers"

Our analysis should be based on rooms with no large objects like tables. Tables in student and adult classrooms are a tremendous waste of valuable space, and they limit the different kinds of teaching methods a group leader can use! Group members sometimes insist on having tables in their classrooms on which they can place their coffee, Bibles, and Personal Study Guides. I've taught Adult Sunday School groups without tables for over twenty years, and members of my groups have managed these items just fine! While tables are certainly convenient for holding personal items like the ones described above, they are expensive in ways far beyond their purchase price.

Consider the actual cost of tables in a classroom. According to Regina Thompson, Studio Director at Visioneering Studios (a church architecture firm), the cost of new educational space is $125–250 per square foot (depending on how complex the project, where it is located, and what the site conditions are like). Each 6-foot rectangular table takes up 15 square feet. If an adult classroom is using four tables to hold coffee and Bibles, the group is using as much as $7,500 worth of space just for tables! Every round table (60 inches diameter) takes up 19 square feet, or $2,375 of space *per table*. In each of these examples, the adult room would hold nine or more additional people without tables present. *These figures are on the low end.* Consider the cost! Are tables more important than people? Education space is expensive to build, and churches have built those spaces to reach and teach people, not to have nice places where members can set their Bibles and coffee cups.

The same is true for items such as couches and pianos. A member in a church I once served donated a used couch for the student ministry. The couch took up 18 square feet, or $2,250 worth of space. While the couch would seat only three students comfortably, the same amount of space held five students comfortably in chairs. A donated piano costs nearly the same. When we maximize our space we maximize the number of people who can attend our Bible teaching ministry.

Another issue with multiple tables in a student or adult classroom is that it limits the types of teaching methods that can be used. Tables and pianos tend to get in the way. Our primary tasks are to reach people, teach people, and connect people to service. Remove anything that hinders these from happening.

Once we measure the space, add to our document the average attendance of the class using a particular room. We can now analyze the space and determine which of our classes are at or near capacity, based on the average attendance and at 80 percent capacity of the room. This helps us to know when to start new classes or when we need to look at moving to multiple Sunday School hours. Keep in mind that as we consider starting new young adult and adult classes, we will need to factor in new or additional classes for preschoolers, children, and students. Many of the new young adults and adults we reach will bring their kids and teenagers with them!

Analysis of the space may show that we need to reassign groups from one room to another. We may discover a small group is occupying a room much larger than is needed, while a larger class is crowded into a smaller room. One solution may be to simply reassign each class to the more appropriate size room. This is why it is important that classes, especially adult classes, not personalize their rooms. It is not unusual to hear "war stories" about teachers and groups who did not want to move to a more size-appropriate room because the group members had purchased and installed curtains, ceiling fans, padded chairs (and in one case, recliners!) or affixed wall art or decorations in their existing room.

We should consider the placement of groups in our buildings. For example, Sunday School classes for young adults should be close to the preschool area. New mothers want to know their babies or preschoolers are nearby in case needs arise to go and check on them. Having classroom space for young adults close to the preschool area also enables parents to securely check their children into their appropriate classrooms and quickly get to their own Bible study locations. Senior or older adults are better served when their classrooms are close to the worship center. Many adults in this age group experience mobility issues, and placing those groups close to the worship center is a way to honor our older members.

Look for non-traditional space on campus, too. A fellowship hall, gymnasium (Family Life Center), bride's room, choir room and even the worship center choir loft can be used for Sunday School space. Look for other unused areas such as the church parlor or even the end of a dead-end hallway. The church library or church offices can be places for people to gather and study God's Word.

Don't forget to use large spaces, such as a fellowship hall or gym. Consider placing multiple classes in the room; when we have three or more classes utilizing one large room, we generate a "buzz" effect so that members of one group don't necessarily hear the conversations and teaching going on in another group. In two churches I served, we had up to seventeen classes on the gym floor, and no one had any issue with the sound or interference from another class.

Though multiple classes generate a "buzz" effect so that sound is not an issue in large spaces like fellowship halls or gyms, people can still be distracted visually. Therefore, consider using partitions to create visual barriers. Those moveable walls also designate the meeting location for each class. For partitions built on site, perhaps by members of the church, place 3-5 inch casters on the bottom frame for ease in moving the partitions each week. We can purchase some casters with a wheel lock so the partitions will be steady once in place. Portable room dividers are also available for purchase from companies such as Screenflex™ or other companies that create free-standing partitions.

Multiple Sunday School Hours

Lack of space should never be a reason to limit the size and scope of our Sunday School. If our Sunday School is almost full, consider starting a second (or third) hour of Sunday School. Growing churches often find it possible to reach more people by having two or more meeting times, without the added cost of building new facilities. Common schedules in a multiple Sunday School format are:

- *Sunday School—Worship—Sunday School*
- *Sunday School & Worship followed by a second hour of Sunday School & Worship*

One common misconception about multiple Sunday Schools is that we double our space. This is not true because preschoolers use their space during both the Sunday School and worship hours. As we reach more millennials or add young adult classes, whether through existing space or multiple Sunday Schools, we need to enlarge our preschool organization and add new groups. As my friend (and Preschool Sunday School teacher) David Francis once wrote,

> "Surprisingly, many churches do not understand that their efforts to grow will be stunted if they don't adequately plan for adding preschool space. Unless new dedicated preschool space can be constructed, this will almost certainly mean that space currently being used for other purposes must be captured for conversion to preschool space. Such space should be on a level that provides safe escape in case of fire. Ideally, it should be near existing preschool space and convenient to the worship center and/or young adult classrooms. In many churches this means that children, students, or adults will be displaced to make room for preschool growth. Such a commitment will pay off in the long term."[50]

Don't Forget Off-Campus Options for Space

Many churches have added space by purchasing adjacent property and utilizing or renovating the space for Sunday School use. Flake conceded that sometimes it is wise to seek what he called "outside space."[51] Student and adult classes often can use houses purchased with little renovation. Other options include renting or leasing adjacent or nearby office space or schools. Adults also can easily use conference rooms, break rooms, lobby areas, and other spaces in office buildings.

An open group strategy such as Sunday School is not limited by where it meets or when it meets. Churches that use a small group strategy have long used group members' homes as locations for their groups. The same can work for a traditional Sunday School model. Adult Sunday School classes can meet off-campus in a member's home or at a location such as a restaurant or coffee shop. For classes meeting off campus on Sunday, however, consider groups whose members have no children or grown children. People who have babies or preschoolers need to be on campus in case an issue arises with their children.

See Through the Eyes of a Guest

We need to walk through our facilities and look at everything through the eyes of a guest who comes to our church on Sunday. Are classrooms clean and free of junk or clutter? Go through the preschool area and make sure rooms are free of unnecessary, broken, old, or unused toys and equipment. Also make sure all the toys and furnishings are clean and sanitized. Smell the room. Make sure you don't notice any lingering offensive odors. Student ministry areas should be orderly and not filled with worn-out furniture or equipment. Adult classrooms should be tidy, carpets should be clean, walls should be painted in neutral colors, and outdated resources (and tables) should be removed. Kids' ministry areas should be neat and welcoming with an atmosphere that says, "we are ready to learn!"

Are restrooms properly cleaned and updated? A church's restrooms are used by a lot of people in 15-20 minute increments. Consider having someone visit each restroom before and during Sunday School to make sure counters are clean and wiped down, all the facilities are working properly, and sufficient paper products are available.

Does clear signage give direction from the parking lot to the building and throughout? Signage should be visible and readable from multiple sight points. Signage suspended from the ceiling works well as individuals can see appropriate directions over the heads of people in a crowded room. Signage should help guests know the location of:

- *Guest Parking*
- *Preschool and Kids Ministries building(s)*
- *Student ministry meeting places*
- *Guest Center*
- *Restrooms*
- *Church offices*
- *Worship Center*

Often we are so familiar with our facilities that we don't realize how difficult it actually is for a guest to navigate our church campuses. One action we may take is to invite someone not familiar with our church facilities to walk through and give feedback. If we are on vacation or away one Sunday, we may find it helpful to attend a church in the area where we are visiting, especially one we have never attended before. Find where to park and what door to enter. Find the Guest Center or where to take a preschooler, child, or student for Sunday School. Locate an appropriate Adult Sunday School class and participate. From there, find the Worship Center. Many people have been surprised at how difficult it is to move through the campus of an unfamiliar church and have returned to their church to suggest appropriate changes in their signage and placement of trained door and hallway greeters.

Don't Forget About Parking

Providing appropriate space includes providing sufficient parking, too. We need to calculate our attendees-per-car ratio. This number will vary from church to church, but it definitely affects how many parking spaces we should have in the parking lot. Many churches have discovered that a single family is driving multiple cars to church. For example, one adult leads a group and needs to arrive earlier than the rest of the family, so he takes one car; a teenager in the family drives her own car, and so on. Sometimes three cars enter the campus from a single family. This leads to challenges as parking spaces fill up. The 80 percent rule applies to our parking lot, too. When the parking lot is 80 percent full, it appears very full to a guest. Churches have discovered that they can create additional parking by parking on the grass or part of the church lawn. These churches develop lanes for cars to enter and exit the grass space with a line of railroad ties or concrete blocks to indicate parking areas or spaces.

Related to parking, we should give consideration to expectant and new mothers and first-time guests. We should provide dedicated parking spaces near the entrance to the preschool area for parents of babies and preschoolers. Parking signs that read "Reserved for Parents of Preschoolers" communicate that our church is serious about reaching young adults. Adequate guest parking should be easily visible and accessible to the worship center and education buildings.

Don't Forget About Resources

Arthur Flake not only recommended providing appropriate space, he also knew that every Bible study class needed resources. Not only do groups need chairs, tables in children's rooms, storage cabinets, and A/V equipment, we should not forget about the one item that is most valuable to provide to groups in whatever space they meet! What is this one piece of "equipment"? It is one of the most important resources a church can place in the hands of members and guests: a study guide that is used by the group to study the Bible systematically. Christian educators are often asked by Sunday School teachers, "Why do we need to use curriculum in our class? Why can't we just study the Bible?" Flake identified three benefits of using "lesson literature," or what we might call ongoing curriculum today. These benefits were having a plan of Bible study, possessing a system of Bible study helps, and provides a vehicle for applying the Bible study to life. [52]

When asked the question, "Why use an ongoing Bible study instead of other options?" Ken Braddy answered like this:

1. Because your goal as a group leader is to make disciples. Discipleship doesn't take a week off, but your group members do! Isn't it a good idea to place in their hands something like a PSG (Personal Study Guide) or the Daily Discipleship Guide so that they have content to read in between attending group studies? This allows them to keep up with the group even when they are not present. Disciples should read God's Word daily, and Personal Study Guides and Daily Discipleship Guides help them do just that.

2. Because the content is trustworthy. Teachers in every church have all kinds of theological backgrounds—some may have been in church for a long time, others not so much. Because we are commanded to guard our doctrine closely, it matters what teachers teach. Turning them loose to teach anything they want opens the door to introducing doctrine into your church that is contrary to your stated beliefs. When you provide an ongoing curriculum for your groups, teachers are held more accountable because both they and their group members have curriculum they are studying. Heresy has almost no chance of surviving when your groups use an ongoing curriculum.

3. Because the Bible studies are carefully crafted by teams of experts. Almost everyone who works on the LifeWay teams I lead have their Ph.Ds in theology or Christian education (or both). We've served on church staffs and state conventions, seminaries, or other institutions. We work in teams to produce/edit the curriculum, and that is a much stronger model than, say, a teacher writing his/her own Bible studies. Think of it like this: "Would you rather your daughter drive a car that one engineer designed, or drive a car that a team of engineers designed?" I'm putting my child in a car built by a team, because there is less chance of a bad design!

4. Because the editors are teachers themselves. Almost without exception, everyone who edits curriculum on my team is a current leader in his or her church's Sunday School or small-group ministry. Because they use the material they produce, they know firsthand if it's working or not, and that helps them tweak things as they go. The editors are great churchmen who are "in the trenches" each week, just like you and the leaders in your church.

5. Because it's very affordable. It is surprising to know that I could equip a teacher with a group box that contains a Leader Guide, a commentary, a Leader Pack (with posters and digital resources that contain the full text of the Leader Guide that the leader can modify for use in class), and ten Personal Study Guides for the teacher's group members all for about $70 every ninety days! If you divide that by the thirteen weeks in the quarter, that's not even $6 a week to equip a group of ten people to study the Bible. To take it to the extreme, it's about $0.56/day...less than a can of Coke!

6. Because you have options. LifeWay offers three major lines of curriculum. One explores the Bible book by book. A second one tackles topics, and the third goes through the Bible chronologically. However a group likes to study the Bible, LifeWay has an option.

7. Because you are reaching guests. By providing curriculum for guests, you help them fit into existing groups. Some guests will not have strong church backgrounds, and attending a Bible study is a big deal. In fact, some guests feel very intimidated to come into groups where everyone appears to have a firm grasp of the Bible. A Personal Study Guide helps guests read ahead and be prepared for class discussion about the Bible.

8. Because your people need balance. Curriculum is designed on a "scope and sequence." The *scope* is the possible topics that could be covered, and *sequence* is the order in which they will be covered. Curriculum providers work hard to make sure that people receive "the whole counsel of God" over time. Sometimes when group leaders prepare their own studies, they gravitate to pet topics and favored doctrines in the Bible. Curriculum ensures that disciples are fed a balanced diet from God's Word over time. [53]

Other Furnishings to Consider

Sunday School classes need other resources and furnishings that will vary by age group. Whereas adults and students are fine with a whiteboard, bulletin board and chairs (with optional TV/ monitor, speaker for mp3 music, and perhaps a podium), preschool and children's areas need specific equipment and furniture based on the primary group using the room. Charts are included in the appendix to help us think through all the furnishings we may need. (See Appendix for Recommended Preschool Equipment and Recommended Equipment for Grades 1-6, pp. 107-109.)

To Arthur Flake, providing space was one of the five basic steps to a balanced and growing Sunday School. The Sunday School that wants to effectively reach people, teach people, and serve people places a priority on providing not only the right amount of space but also the right kind of space. It also expresses its concern for reaching, teaching, and serving by providing adequate and appropriate equipment, furniture, and Bible study resources to help the church achieve her purpose of making disciples.

CHAPTER 7

Go After People

Allan Taylor

Arthur Flake was a man committed to the disciplines necessary for achievement. He was a man intensely devoted to principles. He was a man committed to the process. He was a man who thought strategically, and a man tenacious in execution. He could be perceived as a cold, calculating businessman who transferred his *modus operandi* into his ministry work. Nothing could be further from the truth! He was a man passionate about reaching people. His structures and strategies were just tools needed and used to achieve the desired outcome—reaching people!

As a Bible student, Flake saw the heart of God for the lost and allowed God's heart to become his heart. As with any leader, his life and leadership reflected his personal heart-felt convictions. In his book, *Fuel the Fire: Lessons Learned from the History of Southern Baptist Evangelism,* Dr. Charles S. Kelley, Jr., wrote, "Flake was no fluke." [54] Kelley further stated,

> "A danger arises in ascribing too much attention to any one man. With great accomplishments, a variety of influences will emerge. Nevertheless, some individuals do make outstanding contributions that overshadow the other factors in great deeds or great events. The philosophy of Sunday School work, which has made that institution so productive in evangelism for Southern Baptists, can be understood only by considering the impact of Arthur Flake. ... 'Flake's Formula' has been a major factor in that success for nearly 100 years." [55]

Writing about America's greatest evangelistic force, pastor and author Dr. James Garlow wrote, "The Sunday School Board is known not only for influencing the key evangelistic tool of the Southern Baptists, the Sunday School, but is responsible for a massive literary output unparalleled in any other denomination."[56] Garlow, along with many others, have recognized Sunday School as the "key evangelistic tool" in our churches. Over the decades, many have contributed to the evangelistic thrust of the Sunday School, and Flake would stand among the most influential. One hundred years later, we still feel the impact of his influence!

The Reason for Flake's Formula

We have examined the first four steps of Flake's five-step Formula. The purpose of Flake's previous four steps was to set-up the fifth and final step—reaching people. The first four steps prepared the church for those they were about to receive. These steps are unnecessary if there is no fifth step. Dr. Kelley wrote, "The first four steps are the necessary preparation for growth. Actual growth is the result of going after the people who are the prospects."[57] Churches who have practiced all five steps have found Sunday School to be vibrant, growing, and effective in reaching new people. Flake's Formula postures the church to be more aggressive in evangelism.

We would do well to understand what Flake understood—the number one priority of Sunday School is to witness to the lost, share the gospel, and see people saved! Like a fiery football coach, Flake admonished the leaders of his day, "Prepare the Sunday school to go into action to reach the people. It is time to quit quibbling and dillydallying and get out into the homes and places of business and urge the people to join the Sunday School and attend the services of worship … Every Sunday school should observe a regular visitation program. Nothing else will take its place."[58]

Evangelism in Today's Sunday School

Many today regard Sunday School as irrelevant and antiquated. Sadly, it has become so in many churches. Every organization requires intentional attention and leadership to remain healthy. Sunday School is still the best evangelistic tool the church possesses. Let me share seven reasons this is so.

1. Sunday School is the largest organization in the church. Can you give me a four-letter word why Sunday School is best positioned for evangelistic effectiveness? You may offer "love," or "zeal." But the answer is math! The sheer number of people involved in Sunday School makes it the most potentially evangelistic force the church has.

2. Sunday School meets at "prime time." Sunday School meets when most people are present and when most guests choose to attend.

3. Sunday School is age graded. Now, don't check out on me. Hear me out. The beauty of age grading for evangelistic reasons is so overlooked. We know that age grading is important to the teaching/ learning process but it is also effective when we "go after people." Let me explain. Who in the church will be most effective reaching millennials? Answer: millennials! Who in the church will be most effective reaching baby boomers? Baby boomers! Who in the church will be most effective reaching high schoolers? You guessed it! … high schoolers.

Every Sunday School group is a mission team, or at least it should be. We don't need to form mission teams in the church; we already have them! Let's use the ones we have! Every group should be reaching those in the community who fit their demographic. Flake saw this vision for age grading back in 1923. "Indeed, is not the reason we organize our forces, *grade our schools,* train our officers and teachers, erect our buildings and earnestly seek to win the large numbers into our Sunday schools, that we may win them to Christ?" (emphasis added). [59]

4. Sunday School is for all ages of people. We can pursue everyone because everyone can find his or her place in a Sunday School group regardless of age. Every person of every age needs Jesus. Every person of every age needs to learn the Bible. Every person of every age can find this in Sunday School.

5. Sunday School assimilates new people. The way we reach people is the way we keep people. And the way we keep people is the way we reach people. This begs the question: How do we reach and keep people? With relationships. We don't reach people we don't know and we seldom reach people we barely know. But we can reach people when we have developed some relationship with them. It is natural for people to attend Bible study where there is a pre-existing relationship. Multiple interactions with the unchurched enable us to develop a relationship that becomes our means of assimilation. The way we were able to reach them becomes our way to keep them. A church's outreach strategy should never be divorced from the church's assimilation strategy. The two work hand-in-hand.

6. Sunday School is an open group. Like the sign in the storefront window of a business that flashes "Open," Sunday School is designed to be "open for business," too. That is, anyone is welcome to attend any given session. But it goes deeper than that. Not only is anyone welcome at any time, but an open group is also intentionally and purposefully inviting people to attend its Bible study. Group members make a concerted effort to engage people with an invitation. The hardest time to attend church is the first time, and so it is with Sunday School. The most difficult time to attend is the first time. But it is immensely more stressful to attend a Bible study group the first time than it is to attend a worship service the first time. At least in "big church" we can hide as we blend in with the crowd. Not so with a small group. Many adult groups have slowly and unconsciously become closed. Philosophically they want people to come to their Bible studies and would welcome them if they did. But behaviorally they are doing nothing to engage the unengaged by providing a friendly invitation to attend the group's next Bible study. Flake's response would be, "The number of people on the outside of the Sunday school who should be on the inside would be the true test of a Sunday school's efficiency."[60]

7. Sunday School affords everyone an opportunity to get involved. The church breaks down the daunting task of reaching her community one group at a time. But the group breaks down the task of reaching its prospects one person at a time. Through Sunday School everyone can become involved. Winning people to Jesus is "spiritual hand-to-hand combat." The church needs the hands of every soldier to win the battle, and our Commander in Chief has given each soldier the command, "Go and make disciples" (Matthew 28:18-20). Speaking of a group and its leaders, Flake used a slightly different analogy when he said, "These constitute a soul-winners' band."[61] A musical band with only a handful of instrumentalists will sound pitiful! To produce rich, resonant music, each member of the orchestra must play his or her part. And so it is in Sunday School as Flake pointed out. Everyone can and should be involved in winning people to Jesus. If Flake were alive today he would undoubtedly lead and utilize the Sunday School to "go after people."

Six Essentials for an Evangelistic Sunday School

Sunday School and Evangelism. They have become the odd couple today. Sunday School lost her evangelistic moorings when the church moved from individual evangelism to institutional evangelism.

1. An evangelistic Sunday School must have the example of an evangelistic pastor. Show me an evangelistic church and I will show you an evangelistic pastor. If we want to know the temperature of an organization, then stick the thermometer into the leader's mouth. Nothing in the church rises above the pastor. Pastors need to lead their churches to accomplish the Great Commission. Leading by example is the greatest form of leadership. The challenge of pastoring has never been more difficult and stressful. Pastors are expected to be great theologians, polished communicators, wise counselors, astute organizers, financial gurus, personnel managers, building project managers, and family men; and still have time to visit all the shut-ins. But above all the church activities, a pastor must be intensely focused on seeing people saved. Pastors can delegate many responsibilities to competent staff, faithful deacons, and gifted members; but they cannot afford to pass the leadership of evangelism to anyone else! The pastor must keep his hands on the helm of the evangelistic ship, or it will end up shipwrecked.

2. An evangelistic Sunday School must have a clearly defined vision for evangelism. Sunday School is the perfect strategy to "go after people" as outlined previously in this chapter. But we have destroyed this vision. Not by arguing the pros and cons of evangelism through Sunday School, but by simply ignoring it! Historically, this vision has served the church well. We have forgotten the old cliché: "The main thing is to keep the main thing, the main thing." I am afraid we have become the church going on mission trips instead of the church fulfilling our mission!

Jesus shared His "vision statement" with us.

- "For God did not send his Son into the world to condemn the world, but to save the world through him." (John 3:17)
- "For the Son of Man has come to seek and to save the lost." (Luke 19:10)
- "My food is to do the will of him who sent me and to finish his work [of salvation]." (John 4:34)
- "I have come so that they may have life and have it in abundance." (John 10:10)

Jesus finished His mission.

- "I have glorified you on the earth by completing the work you gave me to do." (John 17:4)
- "... He said, 'It is finished.'" (John 19:30)

Following the example of our Lord, we must have the vision to win the lost and then go finish our mission.

3. An evangelistic Sunday School must enlist teachers and leaders in alignment with this vision. Alignment is an important word for the church. Too often we are unaligned with the truth we preach and believe. If Sunday School is to shoulder the responsibility for evangelism and outreach, then why do we enlist teachers and leaders who are not aligned with this vision? How can we expect to move the evangelistic ball down the field when the quarterback won't call the play? Show me an evangelistic Sunday School group and I will show you an evangelistic group leader. How do we build an evangelistic Sunday School? One group at a time. How do we build evangelistic groups? One leader at a time.

4. An evangelistic Sunday School must have outreach leaders. If preaching is important to the church, then the church needs a preacher. If teaching the Bible is important to the church, then the church needs Bible teachers. If singing is important in the church, then the church needs singers and musicians. If outreach is important to the church then the church needs outreach leaders. Someone has to lead the charge, organize the effort, and execute the necessary details. Every adult group and every preschool, children, and student ministry should have an outreach leader if they are serious about going after people.

The Outreach Leader Job Description

- *Be a personal witness.*
- *Lead the class/department in the outreach/evangelism strategy.*
- *Train class members to share the gospel.*
- *Train class members to share their testimonies.*
- *Train class members in the outreach/evangelism strategy.*
- *Once a month, enlist a member to briefly share a testimony in class of his or her salvation or a witnessing experience.*
- *Keep the class/department Prospect Book updated.*

5. An evangelistic Sunday School must have prospects. If we don't have a name, address, phone number, and/or email address then we don't have a prospect. We don't reach nameless people! Show me a group that has no prospects and I will show you a group that does not intend to reach anyone. Having a list of prospects shows intentionality, and we don't reach people unintentionally!

How do we collect a list of prospects for our group?

- *People who attend our church services*
- *People who visit our Sunday School*
- *Those who attend a special event at our church (Christmas pageant, Easter drama, baptism of a relative, etc.)*
- *Families of children attending our Vacation Bible School*
- *Families of children participating in our church's sports programs*
- *People who come to the church for help with food, clothing, bills, etc.*
- *Family, friends, work associates, schoolmates, and neighbors of church members*
- *People we meet and serve through our church's community involvement*
- *Canvas homes surrounding the church (Flake utilized this greatly).*
- *Conduct a Friend Day or other high attendance strategies.*

6. An evangelistic Sunday School must have an intentional outreach strategy. The word intentional is very important. When we are intentional we are purposeful; we are strategic; we are resolved; we are decisive; we are focused; and we are determined. It's time we get intentional again! Many churches today have no intentional outreach strategy. I find that strange and unnatural. Every organization on earth has an intentional strategy, a method, a plan that is executed in order to accomplish the purpose of the organization. The gospel is much discussed, dissected, and debated but rarely declared. Part of the solution is to provide a tool, a method, a means by which the gospel can be executed. The means for a church is Sunday School, but what is the means for Sunday School? I want to suggest a simple method called the MTV Strategy. MTV stands for **M**ail, **T**elephone, and **V**isit.

MTV

Each month the group contacts its prospects three times. Each prospect receives a monthly hand-written note in the mail, a telephone call, and a visit. The group should coordinate these on different weeks throughout the month.

The MTV strategy has several benefits. First of all, it gives groups an intentional way to cultivate their prospects. MTV also gives the group a systematic way to cultivate prospects throughout the month. A third benefit is seen in prospects receiving three different types of touches over a short period of time which provides opportunities for building relationships. MTV also provides a "hit and stick" strategy as opposed to "hit and run" action. Some people make a one-time contact, hit the prospect with an invitation to church and maybe the gospel, but the prospect never sees them again. The group just executed the "hit and run" method which is a poor way to gain people's trust and be effective in reaching them. Lastly, MTV uses group members where they are usable. People are at different points in their spiritual journey. Many are not ready to make a visit, but most will write a personal note and several will make phone calls. Using people where they are usable allows the group's leadership team to take people where they are and eventually grow them to where they need to be.

How long should a class employ the MTV Strategy with prospects? Every month prospects should continue to receive the three MTV contacts. The process should continue month after month until they attend worship and/or Sunday School; of course the process ends if they tell us to no longer contact them.

Hidden in the Word of God is a great admonition concerning our persistence in reaching the lost. "So (Jesus) told them this parable: 'What man among you, who has a hundred sheep and loses one of them, does not leave the ninety-nine in the open field and go after the lost one *until he finds it?*'" (Luke 15:3-4, emphasis added).

"'Or what woman who has ten silver coins, if she loses one coin, does not light a lamp, sweep the house, and search carefully *until she finds it?*'" (Luke 15:8, emphasis added).

To "go after people" was the chief aim of Jesus and the early church. It is to be the chief aim of the Sunday School. This too, was the chief aim of Arthur Flake's vision for Sunday School. "Christ's mission to this world was to win souls; that was the purpose of his coming. The Apostle Paul said, 'Christ Jesus came into the world to save sinners,' and should not we also in all our Sunday schools have this as our supreme aim?"[62]

May we, too, *Go After People!*

CHAPTER 8

Building a Standard Sunday School

David Francis

In the Field or From the Office?

"Perhaps the most difficult question constantly facing the department [of Sunday School Administration] is the balancing of time between office promotion and field work." ('34:301) [63]

That's how Arthur Flake described the tension of attending requests for training from the field in his thirteenth annual report as the first Director ("Secretary") of the Department of Sunday School Administration. It was a part of the official report of the Baptist Sunday School Board (BSSB) presented each year to the Southern Baptist Convention. He submitted fifteen such reports (1921–1936), which are the sources for most of this chapter. His name first appears in the 1909 report as joining the team of "Field Secretaries." [64] He likely assumed it had been noted for the last time in the 1919 report ('19:468):

> During the year, however, Mr. Arthur Flake, who for nearly ten years had been the Field Secretary for the B.Y.P.U. west of the Mississippi, resigned to take up other work. [65]

Perhaps it was the same question that prompted Flake to take a break in denominational service to lead one church's education ministry from an office at First Baptist Church Fort Worth, Texas. That "other work" did not last long, as the 1920 report notes:

> During the last year we have added ... the Department of Sunday School Administration, under the direction of Mr. Arthur Flake ... The Department ... has just been organized, and has not yet fully begun its work. Through this department we hope to systematize the work of the Superintendents, the Secretaries and the Treasurers, and to

facilitate the work of organization. We hope through this department to be able to get in touch with those who work in Sunday-school organizations and to standardize methods and material. The announcement of this department has already created a great deal of interest. As part of its work, the *Superintendent's Quarterly* will be changed into a monthly and will be made the exponent for the work of the department. We count this one of the most far-reaching of our recent plans, and we confidently believe that it will work a revolution in our methods. [66]

Equipping Officers as Well as Teachers

Nearly from its outset, the Baptist Sunday School Board (BSSB) had set forth a strategy not just to produce Bible lessons, but to equip Sunday School teachers to teach with excellence. A thorough system had been developed by the Education[al] department under the leadership of P.E. Burroughs, architect of many of the BSSB's early innovations (including the architecture department!). By early 1918, teachers had earned almost 45,000 diplomas, along with red, blue, and gold seals; and over 100,000 book awards. Almost all of this activity was by teachers and in the "normal" courses. [67]

I. The Normal Courses for Teacher Training

1. The Convention Normal Course

2. The Post-Graduate Normal Course

II. The Certificate Courses

1. The Lecture Course with Certificate

2. The Reading Course (with Certificate)

3. The General Recognition Certificate

III. The Standards of Excellence

1. The A-1 Standard

2. The AA-1 Standard

3. Class Standards

4. Departmental Standards

IV. Standard Church and Sunday School Buildings

The creation of the Administration department with Arthur Flake at its helm was an effort to provide Sunday School officers a system of training similar to that available to Sunday School teachers through the Educational Department. There was more demand for such help than could possibly be satisfied by personal trainers. In that day, it was not uncommon for executives to fulfill field training requests, as well as a growing number of state Sunday School [directors], and lay persons who had demonstrated expertise and were being trained to train. Still, not enough people were available to train everyone personally.

The Administration System

Flake and his team took on the challenge this void presented by developing a system for training Sunday School officers—especially the superintendent (director)—that supplemented or substituted for live field personnel. It had these components:

Enlargement campaigns. Typically eight intense days long—Sunday to Sunday. These could involve one church, an association, or a wider area with state convention help. The churches would literally do the five steps in Flake's Formula in a week's time, emerging on the second Sunday with new classes, new teachers, and new enrollees. Flake considered these the best use of field personnel in terms of ROI (return on investment).

Large Conferences and Clinics. Held maybe once or twice a year with broad geographical appeal, conferences could last several days, while clinics could last several weeks. Both required state sponsorship.

Superintendents' meetings. These were typically two-day events. Flake's team discovered that fully one-third of all Sunday School directors were new each year. It was difficult to reach them for training. Near the end of his tenure, Flake's department executed an effort to simply get the names and contact information on directors, so that they could offer them literature and other helps.

Free literature. The department published dozens of brief pamphlets on various specific organizational topics. Some were packaged by topic.

A monthly publication. *The Sunday School Builder* was a monthly resource. It was the key periodical for enforcing and spreading the department's work. That work included a growing movement of church-based libraries and the promotion of daily Vacation Bible School, which was housed in the department until it became its own. Circulation grew from 7,000 in 1920 to over 20,000 by 1928. [68]

Emphasizing the Standards. Flake's hallmark book, *Building a Standard Sunday School* is more a commentary on the Standard than an introduction of it—although for most it served both purposes. Some terms are changed in the book compared with earlier versions of the Standard. So Flake certainly put his mark on the checklist—one that is compatible with "Flake's Formula." But neither is derived from the other. And both are helpful. Flake began his first annual report with that emphasis:

> Increasing interest is constantly being manifested in the Standards of Excellence. A continuous stream of inquiries has been coming to our office concerning both Standards. Two hundred and forty-five schools reached the First Standard, and the number of Advanced Standard Schools is double that of the preceding year. [69]

The First Standard called for:

> **Church Control.** The church shall elect officers and teachers; the school shall make monthly or quarterly reports to the church.

> **Enrollment** shall equal the number of resident church members.

> **Graded.** The school shall be graded [into eight departments].

Baptist literature shall be used in the school.

Bible usage. Used by at least 75 percent of leaders and pupils.

Preaching attendance. 75 percent of Sunday School attendance above 8 years old.

Evangelism. The school shall be positively evangelistic.

Weekly Teachers' Meeting or Monthly Workers' Conference. Attended by at least 50 percent of teachers and leaders.

Normal Course Diplomas. 50 percent of the teachers and officers … shall hold a Convention Normal Course Diploma.

Denominational Work. Four of the general causes presented annually with contributions collected.

The Advanced Standard added stringent requirements for department structure, building provision, working equipment, etc. Few churches ever applied for this certification. In fact, "twice as many" cited above is two churches instead of one.

The number of churches that achieved these standards during Flake's tenure can be found on the chart: Number of Standard Sunday Schools (Appendix, p. 110).

Associational work. As the system developed, more and more effort was placed on helping "district associations." An Associational "Standard" was developed. Only a relative few associations earned the distinction of being "standard." But those that did had a disproportionately large percentage of the "standard" churches and enjoyed far and away the strongest growth in Sunday School. Flake also strengthened partnerships with "State Sunday School secretaries." Examine the chart on page 110 to determine where that practice was most successful.

Associational Sunday School Standard

I. Officers

1. The officers shall be an associational superintendent, secretary-treasurer, and a group superintendent for each group.

2. The Association shall be divided into two or more groups of churches according to their accessibility. There shall not be over ten churches in any one group.

II. Meetings

1. There shall be held a monthly meeting of the associational officers.

2. There shall be held monthly under the direction of the associational superintendent a meeting for all the Sunday School workers in the Association. Fifty percent of the schools shall be represented by at least one general officer.

III. Reports.

1. Fifty percent of the Sunday School superintendents shall make a monthly report to the associational superintendent, and this report must be in the hands of the associational superintendent at least three days before the monthly meeting.

2. The associational superintendent shall make a monthly report to the state Sunday School Department.

IV. Extension and Enlargement

1. There shall be a Sunday School in every co-operating church in the Association as reported by letter to the Association, or to the state secretary, for the calendar year.

2. Twenty-five percent of the schools shall take a religious census each calendar year and the information shall be used in an effort to build up the membership of the school.

V. Standardization

1. Fifty per cent of the schools in the Association shall be Standard schools, according to the Standard of Excellence of the Baptist Sunday School Board.

A Curriculum: The Course in Sunday School Administration. Sunday School officers were encouraged to work toward certification in this course. Officers could gain recognition by reading six books and completing study questions at the end of each chapter. Options developed for books 3 and 5 over time. This chart is from 1934.[70]

Books. Alone or as a part of a system, books were key training tools. Officers could earn certificates and seals by reading the books and submitting answers to the study questions included in most of them. Flake eventually wrote or co-wrote six of the books that were part of the Course in Sunday School Administration. (See Appendix for Chart: Awards by Book Title (1934) and Chart: Rewards Earned by Book (1925-1935), pp. 111-112.)

Libraries. The church library movement ignited and was fueled by Flake's department. The simple exhortation was threefold: build a church library, put the right books in it, and get workers to read them.

A Chief Book: Arthur Flake's book, *Building a Standard Sunday School,* was completed more than all the others put together. It was the key book in the system.

Did it Work?

Fewer than five percent of the 20,000-plus Southern Baptist Sunday Schools were ever recognized as "Standard" in any year. Some 75 percent never applied for such recognition. Yet, in Flake's own words, "It is quite evident from the results in the few Sunday schools that have used the Standard consecutively for a period of years that the usual criticisms are not well founded."[71]

"If any defense of this instrument [the Standard] of Sunday School promotion should be needed, it is easily found in the results which come to those churches which have Standard Sunday Schools. The average Sunday School membership of the South: 72 for every 100 [resident] church members. In the churches which have Standard Sunday Schools, there is twenty percent more result in evangelism proportionately in churches having Standard Sunday Schools. The Standard establishes right relationship between the Sunday school and the church of which it is a part, places its central emphasis on Bible teaching and soul-winning, and constantly develops a well wounded program of Sunday School work." [72]

The Standards of Excellence, as well as the books that told how to achieve them, and the events that rallied people to act on them had an impact on many more churches than those that could put a check mark by every item in the standard, read and secure credit for every book, and apply for recognition every year. (See Appendix for Chart: Impact of Achieving Sunday School Standard Recognition, p. 113.) Flake was uncompromising when it came to principles and processes. But the purpose was always people.

People

Flake was about people. The last step in his formula exhorts us to "go after the people." For his team, he chose good people. His two associates went on to greater leadership positions. Harold E. Ingraham, who succeeded Flake, later became the business manager for the Baptist Sunday School Board. J. N. Barnette next led an expanded Sunday School department, giving leadership to all the field functions. Ingraham began the 1937 report with this paragraph:

Mr. Arthur Flake

In this first report since the retirement of Mr. Flake last June, the rest of us in the department desire to express our whole-souled love and appreciation for this great man who did so much for Southern Baptist Sunday school work and who was secretary of this department from its inception in 1920. No word of ours could be adequate here as his contribution can never be fully revealed. We do, however, express our most grateful appreciation for what he has meant to each of us personally and to the great task which we have. [73]

For whatever his department accomplished, Flake shared the credit. Because of his reports, we know that the busy phones in the department were answered by department assistant Miss Emma Noland. [74] And that Miss Leona Lavender, who established the church library work, married a Louisville pastor and became Mrs. C. B. Althof. [75]

A Personal Word

Flake died in 1952. I was born in 1952. It was my privilege to serve in a role at LifeWay very similar to his. The key difference was that he had no accountability for Sunday School curriculum. But we shared the ownership of the other big Sunday School numbers. And a stubbornness about the big Sunday School principles. We both loved the people who carry the burden for Sunday School in the state conventions. We both saw the promise of what might happen if associational leaders kindled a fire for Sunday School. His idea of "group leaders" for a set of 5-10 churches in an association remains brilliant. As my friend Bob Mayfield, the author of the next chapter and "State Sunday School Secretary" in Oklahoma, had emblazoned on coffee cups for a [yet!] annual meeting of the state directors, "Arthur Flake is my Homeboy." I'm not even completely sure what that means! But I think it at least means "we're in this together." Reading some other documents, Flake may have been taking some "friendly fire" when he retired. Flake's successor. J. N. Barnette— famous for conceiving "A Million More in '54"—did likewise. Harry Piland. Bill Taylor. Allan Taylor. Ken Braddy. To all these men goes thanks from the depths of my heart for holding up the banner of Sunday School. Even when it felt like the famous scene from Iwo Jima. May you be inspired by Arthur Flake—as we are and were—to help lift the banner of Sunday School high again.

CHAPTER 9

Arthur Flake's Legacy

Bob Mayfield

It has been 100 years since Arthur Flake started his historic, pioneering ministry at the Baptist Sunday School Board. When Flake began his ministry in Nashville, here are some of the headlines and trends:

- *The 19th Amendment was ratified, giving women the right to vote.*
- *An English expedition uncovered the tomb of Egyptian King Tutankhamen.*
- *Edward, Prince of Wales was an icon in men's fashion, sporting "plus fours," an adaptation of men's knickers.*
- *"The Charleston" was the dance craze of the decade.* [76]
- *The National Football League began in 1920*
- *The Model T was the most popular automobile in America*
- *A gallon of gasoline was 30 cents*
- *Median price of a house was $3,200*
- *A quart of milk was 9 cents.* [77]

It is doubtful Arthur Flake could picture our world today, where a smart phone can access virtually any information in the world in seconds, where one can travel anywhere in the world in less than 24 hours, and man has walked on the moon! The most common photograph of Flake shows a somber man in his 60's toward the end of his career, with balding hair, and a 3-piece business suit. (See p. 10) What we do not see in that photograph is a man full of vision and dreams. Arthur Flake had a passion to evangelize the lost and make disciples.

Arthur Flake was a man with a unique combination of skills. He was a man who could see the big picture, dream a better picture, and implement a plan to get there. Few people have both the visionary and implementation skills. Flake had both, and his unique ability to both design and build still impacts the Sunday School and small group movement today. The formula developed by Arthur Flake 100 years ago impacts pastors and leaders in churches today, many of whom have never heard Flake's name.

Flake's Impact Today ...

Rick Warren grew a mega-church in southern California by implementing Flake's plan. In his book, *The Purpose Driven Church*, [78] Warren shares how he implemented the first principle of Flake's Formula (Know Your Possibilities) by doing door-to-door surveys and asking people about their needs, followed with an invitation to church. Using this information, Warren designed "Saddleback Sam" so that his church could define their possibilities.

The second principle in Flake's Formulas is Enlarge the Organization. As we have already shown, starting new groups is essential to reaching new people with the gospel. The simple but profound effort to start new groups is essential to evangelizing people and growing churches. New groups are essential for any church, regardless of size or location. Under the leadership of Pastor Kevin Baker, Martha Road Baptist Church in Altus, Oklahoma has grown from 40 to almost 300 in 14 years. The church's secret: two to three new groups are consistently started every year. It is not uncommon today to hear of larger churches that begin over 100 groups every year!

The next stop in Flake's Formula focuses on leadership. We can give Flake credit for many positive contributions, but there is no doubt that one of the greatest contributions he made to advance the gospel was his role in leading leaders. Flake was not content to simply give a leader a book and let him teach from it; he knew the person had to lead a group of people. Therefore, a trained leader is essential to the plan. In the chapter about enlisting and training leaders, Steve Parr provided excellent research about the value of training leaders. The fact is that churches that regularly equip their small group and Sunday School leaders are more likely to grow. Churches that refuse to equip their leaders are likely to decline.

Many churches provide their own video training. Other churches use email. With today's online resources and a smart phone, training for any Sunday School leader is literally at the fingertips of almost any leader in America.

Space is vital to a growing Sunday School ministry. Note that the fourth point of Flake's Formula does not say "build space." Instead, it says "provide space." Groups need space in order to grow, and the more groups a church has the more space it needs. But you can find alternatives to building space. Restaurants, schools, movie theaters, and businesses make tremendous locations for off-campus groups to meet. The home group movement emphasizes having groups that meet in, well … homes! Using off-campus space can be a permanent solution depending on the church's needs and vision. But off-campus space can be a temporary solution to buy time if the church's context requires an on-campus building. Also, many church members appreciate the vision and creativity of their leaders when off-campus space is used. Rather than being a detriment, most people respond well when the church creatively addresses its space issues. Many people would rather attend off-campus groups.

The final piece of Flake's Formula is lifted straight out of Scripture and the Great Commission to "Go." Evangelism was Arthur Flake's driving force and he recognized the value and role that Sunday School can play in introducing people to God's Word. Flake believed in the positive impact Christians could have in evangelizing the lost. Groups of believers offer the opportunity for people to ask questions and converse with each other about Jesus Christ. In fact, as Acts 4:12 states about Jesus, "There is salvation in no one else, for there is no other name under heaven given to people by which we must be saved." The more we talk about Jesus in our Bible study group, especially when lost friends and neighbors are present, the greater number of them will commit to follow Jesus as one of His disciples.

A Sunday School class or small group is a fantastic environment to introduce lost people to Christ. A small class of people is a great place for someone to "kick the tires" of Christianity. Most people do not buy a car without a test drive, or a house without an inspection. People far from God instinctively know that making Christ the Lord of their lives is the major decision they face in this world. They need an environment where they can inspect Jesus Christ for themselves and ask questions about the gospel. In a day when Billy Sunday drew thousands to his events, Arthur Flake went the opposite direction by equipping the saints to do the work of the ministry, emphasizing outreach and evangelism.

In the previous chapter, David Francis mentioned a coffee mug that was distributed at a LifeWay meeting. The mug had a picture of Arthur Flake with the caption, "Arthur Flake is My Homeboy." On the reverse side of the mug, each principle of Flake's Formula was listed. The previous year, T-shirts with the same picture and caption were given to the men and women who lead their state Sunday School ministries. A LifeWay employee stated, "Unfortunately, outside of the people currently in this building, I doubt there are more than 500 people on the planet who know about Arthur Flake."

Although his observation may or may not have been accurate, the point is that Arthur Flake's vision of Sunday School does impact our world today, and even though a person may not know who Flake is, it does not minimize his impact. The question is not really about who does or does not know about Flake. Arthur Flake has impacted thousands of churches, tens of thousands of small groups, and millions of people; and he has changed the eternal destiny of untold numbers of people. So, what about …

The Next 100 Years

Who is going to be the next Arthur Flake? Who will be that person of vision, creativity, and persistence that is going to put everything on the line to bring men and women, boys and girls, grandmas and grandpas, into a personal relationship with Jesus Christ? Who is going to lead their church or lead their group to make disciples and carry out the Great Commission in their context? Who is going to share the gospel, fight the good fight of faith, and finish the course? Who will stand in this moment of time and be a man or a woman of whom this world is not worthy? Who is going to set the course for others for the next 100 years?

How about you?

"Me?" Yes, how about you? Okay, I can honestly assure you that you will *not* be the next Arthur Flake. God has already created an Arthur Flake. The world will never have another Arthur Flake. What the world needs is *you*. God didn't create you to be someone else. He created you to be you, and He has given you spiritual gifts, His Spirit, and experiences that He wants to use in His church. Throughout history, when God needed a champion, He raised up a man or woman to meet the need. Think of them: Noah, Abraham, Moses, Joshua, Deborah, David, Jeremiah, Esther, Mary, Peter, John, and Paul. Remember that these were ordinary men and women. They included nomads, shepherds, common folk, mothers, fishermen, and tentmakers. Arthur Flake was a salesman! You may be saying, "What can I do?" With God's Spirit, strength, and leadership, more than you might think. But it starts with being who you are, not trying to be someone else.

Five Ideas for Leaders of the Groups Movement

1. Nurture Your Soul. This is about God, not you! Resist the urge to read your press clippings, and read your Bible instead. We live in a world where Bibles are abundant, but Bible reading is rare. The average person is unaware that he or she lives in a world that wants to steal your soul. Every minute of every day, the devil is looking for an unlocked door so that he can steal your soul. "A thief comes only to steal, kill, and destroy. I have come that they may have life and have it in abundance" (John 10:10). The enemy usually does not steal your soul all at once. He starts by stealing it one little piece at a time. "We demolish arguments and every proud thing that is raised up against the knowledge of God, (*how?*) and we take every thought captive to obey Christ" (2 Cor. 10:4b-5).[79] Guard your soul by being a student of God's Word. Capture His Word in your heart, and pray. God's Word helps us recognize when God is speaking to us, and when the enemy is trying to steal another piece of our soul.

2. Start Small. Avoid the temptation to go big right from the start. Arthur Flake did not start his ministry as the Sunday School leader of the largest protestant denomination in America. He started with his Sunday School class. He discipled young people in Winona, Mississippi. Arthur Flake grew into the man and the ministry God had for him. The same is true of us. Every experience we have, good or bad, is used by God to grow us into the person and the ministry He has in store for us. "He who started a good work in you will carry it on to completion until the day of Christ Jesus" (Phil. 1:6).

3. Make Disciples. Consider Jesus' ministry during His time on this planet. Jesus did not go big; instead, He went small. He started with a small group of twelve men. Jesus invested himself in the twelve. Jesus' disciple-making plan is evident in Luke 8, 9, and 10. In Luke 8, Jesus modeled ministry for His disciples. In essence, He was saying, "Watch. See what I did there? See how I did ministry here?" People most often model what they see their leader doing. In chapter 9, He sent the disciples out with simple instructions to do what they had previously seen him do. He gave the same instructions in Luke 10. However, then He did not send just twelve disciples, but He "appointed seventy-two others" (v. 1). His disciples multiplied and produced more disciples.

Disciple-making was the essential component of Flake's ministry. Flake's Formula simply will not be as effective if the disciple-making component is not there. The church might start a new group or two and have a big vision for a season, but long, sustained growth will not occur without discipling new leaders. Remember that step three of Flake's Formula is to Enlist and Train Leaders. As the leader of a small group or the point-person of a church's small group organization, it is imperative that we multiply ourselves. It is just as imperative that our leaders multiply themselves also.

Here is a vital concept to us, our leaders, our small groups, and our church: *You cannot grow a strong church with weak disciples.* It just can't be done. Growing a strong church with weak disciples is like running a marathon with emphysema. The lungs can't produce enough oxygen to fuel the body to run the race. We may get a few yards from the starting line, but it's doubtful we will go far in the race.

Multiplication is the common ingredient in Kingdom growth. As a person who leads a small group or a discipleship group, or someone who leads the church's small group organization like the pastor or other staff member, it is vital that we multiply ourselves as leaders. It is also vital that the church multiply its disciples by increasing the number of small groups. Chapter 4 addressed how to multiply groups.

4. Be an Evangelist. The apostle Paul instructed his young protégé, Timothy, to "do the work of an evangelist" (2 Tim. 4:5). Paul recognized that the gospel was always one generation from extinction. We must teach evangelism, and pass the torch down to the next generation. It is sad that in many churches, the Sunday School suffers because its members are not actively sharing their faith with others. Arthur Flake concluded that evangelism must be the primary work of the Sunday School. Sunday School groups offer a rich environment for evangelism, if the group leaders and members understand that their groups are supposed to be outwardly focused. Our purpose should be less about ourselves and more about reaching people who do not know God. Our groups exist to introduce people to Jesus so they can begin walking with Him.

Groups talk about what they are passionate about. Groups that have lots of fellowship together naturally talk about their fellowship. Groups that engage in service projects together discuss their service. Groups tell stories. Groups that are sharing the gospel with their friends, relatives, acquaintances, and neighbors have evangelistic stories to tell. These stories surface naturally in the conversations within the group.

It is critical that group leaders share stories with our groups when we have gospel conversations in our daily activities. People model their leaders. Group members often develop a passion for evangelism because they see their leader's heart for spiritually lost people. We should take group members with us when we visit guests or neighbors so that they can see how we work the gospel into our conversations. Have different people share their testimonies during group time (this gives them practice in a safe environment, and who knows—a lost person might be in the group that day who is reached through the group member's testimony). Take opportunities to teach the gospel so that group members know what they believe.

And teach your group a gospel presentation—a simple one—they can share with others on a moment's notice.

5. Keep it Simple and Sustainable. Whatever process or pathway we choose to make disciples and build the Bible study organizations in our churches, keep it simple and keep it sustainable. The more complex our system becomes, the more difficult it becomes for the average person to understand and pass along. If a church member does not understand the system, it will almost guarantee that they are not going to be excited about it. When was the last time we were excited about something we did not understand?

In addition to keeping things simple, the process also needs to be sustainable. This principle means that the process must work smoothly when the leader is not there supervising everything. The higher the sophistication and the greater the need for supervision, the more likely it is that the system will fail.

The real beauty of Arthur Flake's Formula was and still is its simplicity and sustainability. It's just five simple steps that any church anywhere and of any size can do. Flake's Formula is sustainable. After a church or group has gone through the five steps of Flake's Formula, hit repeat and do it again. And again. And again.

Flake's Formula still works today. We may use different terminology, such as "groups" instead of "units" and "leaders" instead of "teachers," but the principles remain the same. May we continue to reach new people with the gospel through our small group Bible studies using Arthur Flake's simple, but sustainable "formula."

Genesis of Flake's Formula

Flake's Notes	Building a Standard Sunday School (1922)	Flake's Formula (recognized)
1. Find out who should belong	I. The Constituency for the Sunday School Should Be Known.	1. Know the possibilities
2. Assort, grade, and tabulate	II. The Organization Should Be Enlarged.	2. Enlarge the organization
3. Enlarge the organization	III. A Suitable Place Should Be Provided.	3. Enlist and train workers
4. Grade the Sunday School	IV. The Enlarged Organization Should Be Set Up.	4. Provide space and resources
5. Go after them	V. A Program of Visitation Should Be Maintained.	5. Go after the people

Meeting Space Recommendations

Age Group	Space per Person	Maximum Enrollment	Room Size	Leader: Learner Ratio
Preschool				
Babies	35 sq. ft.	12	420 sq. ft.	1:2
Ones-Twos	35 sq. ft.	12	420 sq. ft.	1:3
Threes-Pre-K	35 sq. ft.	16	560 sq. ft.	1:4
Kindergarten	35 sq. ft.	20	700 sq. ft.	1:5
Children				
Younger Kids	25 sq. ft.	20	600 sq. ft.	1:6
Older Kids	20 sq. ft.	24	480 sq. ft.	1:6
Students				
Gr. 7-12 (class)	12-15 sq. ft.	16	192-240 sq. ft.	1:8
Adults				
Class	15-18 sq. ft.	20-32	300-576 sq. ft.	1:4
Special Education				
Low-functioning	25 sq. ft.	6	480 sq. ft.	1:1
High-functioning		15	(+10 sq. ft. per	1:4
In between		12	person for wheelchairs)	1:2-1:3

Recommended Preschool Equipment

Symbols: x – recommended; o – optional; all – for use by all ages

General	B	1	2	3	4	K	All	B-2	3-K	B-5
Rest mats or towels	x	x	o					x		O
Cribs (hospital 27"x42" - must meet federal guidelines)	x	o						x		X
Adult rocking/glider chair (2)	x							x		X
Solid surface floor mat (42"x42")	x									
Wall cabinet (50" above floor)	x	x	x	x	X	x		x	x	X
Trash receptacles with lid	x	x	x	x	X	x		x	x	X
Diaper bag cubbies or hooks	x	x	x							
Vinyl changing pad		x	x							
Open shelf/closed back for toys (26"x37"x12")		o						o		O
Child safety gate										O
Water source for disinfecting	x	x	x					x		X
Slow cookers	x							x		X
Folding screen for nursing area	x							x		X
Rocking boat with enclosed steps		o								
Small countertop refrigerator	o									
Home living/Dramatic Play										
Horizontal unbreakable mirror 24"x28" attached to wall	x	x						o		
Vertical, unbreakable mirror 24"x48" attached to wall			x	x	X	x			o	O
Wooden doll bed (16"x28"x8")		o	x	x	X	x		x	x	X
Child size rocker		o	x	x	X	x			x	X
Table (24"x36"x22")				x	X					
Table (24"x36"x24")				x	X				x	X
2-4 chairs (10")				x						
2-4 chairs (12"-14")			x	x	X				x	X
Wooden sink			x	x	X	x			x	X
Chest of drawers					x					
Child size ironing board and play iron							o			
Music										
CD Player	x	x	x	x	X	x		x	x	X
Autoharp							x			
Rhythm instruments							x			
Blocks										
Cardboard or vinyl blocks		x	x					x		
Wooden unit blocks (various shapes/sizes) 29-70				x					x	X
Wooden unit blocks (various shapes/sizes) 100-150					X	x				
Open shelf/closed back (26"x36"x12")			o	x	X	x			x	X
Art										
Table (30"x48"x22")				x	x				x	X
Table (30"x48"x24")					X	x				
2-4 chairs (10")				x	x					
2-4 chairs (12"-14")					X	x			o	O
Art Easel/adjustable legs*			x	x	X	x			o	O
Drying rack			x	x	X	x			x	X
Water source at child's height for clean up			x	x	X	x			x	X
Art shelf (36"x46"x16")					x					

Recommended Preschool Equipment (cont.)

Nature/Science	B	1	2	3	4	K	All	B-2	3-K	B-5
Open shelf with closed back (26"x36"x12")				x	X	x			o	O
Water/table (1 per church)							o			
Table (24"x36"x24")					O					
Manipulatives/Puzzles										
Puzzle Rack				o	O	o			o	O
Table (24"x36"x24")						o				
2-4 chairs (12"-14")						o				

Source: *Kids Ministry 101: Practical Answers to Questions About Kids Ministry* (Nashville: LifeWay Press, 2009).

Maximum number of two tables per room in 2-4 year old rooms.

*One option for art easels would be to have one easel per every three rooms.

Recommended Equipment for Grades 1-6

Symbols: x – recommended; o - optional

Equipment	Recommended or Optional	Size
Chairs (age-appropriate size)	x	Grades 1 & 2: 12-13 inches Grades 3 & 4: 14-15 inches Grades 5 & 6: 16-17 inches
Coat rack	x	
Resources cabinet	x	
Tables	x	Tabletops for children should be 10 inches above chair seats
Shelves	x	14-19 inches deep, 42-26 inches high, and 3-4 ft long, with shelves 12-14 inches apart.
Book racks	x	42-46 inches high, and 30-42 inches long
Bulletin Board	x	24-30 inches in height and 6-10 feet in length, with the bottom edge 24-30 inches above the floor
Wastebasket	x	
Sink	x	
TV/Monitor/DVD Player	o	
CD Player	o	
Piano	o	
Marker Board(s)	x	
Tear sheets	x	
Felt-tip markers	x	
Other art/writing supplies	x	
Picture rails	x	Picture rails should be about 30 inches above the floor on the front wall and 12 feet long

Source: *Kids Ministry 101: Practical Answers to Questions About Kids Ministry* (Nashville: LifeWay Press, 2009).

Number of Standard Sunday Schools (1920-1933)													
	'20	'21	'22	'23	'24	'25	'26	'27	'28	'29	'30	'31	'32	'33
AL	9	13	15	8	10	18	19	32	54	72	100	131	142	121
AR	2	11	4	8	11	15	12	16	9	10	16	23	17	20
FL	2	2	5	4	5	7	12	23	26	25	30	30	21	23
GA	5	10	20	16	16-5	23	34	61	54	50	55	50	39	36
IL	3	1	3	3	1	1	3	5	5	5	6	11	14	16
KY	21	15	22	28	33	62	82	92	86	76	102	87	106	111
LA	1	2	4	12	29	69	97	135	159	161	114	87	78	60
MD	0	0	1	2	1	1	3	2	4	2	2	1	2	4
MS	16	13	14	9	10	24	24	31	19	29	35	35	33	23
MO	3	2		9	19	24	25	34	18	23	19	23	29	32
NM	3	9	78	4	8	9	6	10	8	12	14	11	10	11
NC	15	18	24	32	43	91	115	140	137	127	133	125	113	82
OK	7	8	8	10	11	19	24	21	22	23	28	31	26	20
SC	1	2	1	6	15	34	48	62	47	46	57	67	54	34
TN	2	8	9	6	7	17	20	27	13	11	13	16	13	14
TX	33	66	92	89	87	112	167	174	177	227	278	280	275	253
VA	2	6	6	5	10	19	25	33	29	25	29	36	37	38
TOT	125	186	243	251	315	545	686	898	867	924	1,031	1,044	1,010	898

Compiled from annual reports presented to the Southern Baptist Convention by the Baptist Sunday School Board (now LifeWay)

Awards by Book Title (1931)

	Book Title	Author(s)	NUMBER
1	Building a Standard Sunday School	Flake	13,407
2	Sunday School Officers and Their Work	Flake	771
3	The Department Sunday School	Flake & Blankinship	272
	The Rural & Village Sunday School	Flake & Lavender	813
4	The Sunday School Secretary & the Six Point Record System	Flake & Noland	722
	The Sunday School & the Church Budget	Flake	326
5	How to Plan Church Buildings	Burroughs	107
	The Church Library	Lavender	69
	Associational Sunday School Work	Barnette	163
6	The True Functions of the Sunday School	Flake	5,321
	TOTAL		21,971

Source: 1935 Southern Baptist Convention Annual, page 318. (https://www.sbhla.org/sbc_annuals/)

Awards Earned by Book as Reported in SBC Annual

	1	2	3		4	5				6	
	Bldg SSS	SS Off	Dept SS	RV SS	SS Sec	How Plan	SS & Budg	Library	Assoc SS	True Funct	TOTALS
'25	20,500	6,000	3,600		7,500						38,800#
'26	18,340	2,266	1,353	121	3,228	297					25,605
'27*											
'28	18,969	1,015	552	598	1,498	278					22,910
'29	15,247	1,624	962	1,624	1,642	359				1,349	21,188
'30	15,105	1,523	673	725	1,409	1,970				2,779	22,560
'31*											
'32	10,663	753	316	523	1,058	351				3,216	16,880
'33	8,957	1,052	399	1,217	902	381				3,297	16,205
'34	13,497	771	272	813	722	107	326	69	163	5,321	21,971
'35	38,119	1,117	234	289	406	101				1,779	42,166
TOT	159,397	16,121	8,361	5,910	18,365	4,301				17,741	189,485

*not reported in SBC Annual   #circulation

Compiled from reports included in Southern Baptist Annuals, 1926-1936

Impact of Achieving Standard Sunday School Recognition

Achieved Standard for...	# churches	Church membership	SS enrollment
15 consecutive years (1919-1933)	9	92% gain	96% gain
10-14 years consecutively (11 years avg.)	76	50% gain	54% gain
5-9 years consecutively (8 years avg.)	492	40% gain	40% gain

Source: 1935 Southern Baptist Convention Annual, p. 317 (https://www.sbhla.org/sbc_annuals/)

ENDNOTES

1. Arthur Flake, *Building a Standard Sunday School* (Nashville: Convention Press, 1922), 103.

2. All Scripture quotations, unless otherwise noted, will be in CSB translation.

3. John Milburn Price, ed., *Baptist Leaders in Religious Education* (Nashville: Broadman Press, 1943), 57.

4. *The Circle*, August 1952, 5.

5. LaGrange, Fayette County website. http://www.fayettecountyhistory.org/la_grange.htm.

6. "Arthur Flake, Sunday School Pioneer, Dies at Age of 90 in Memphis," *Baptist Press*, July 3, 1952, http://media.sbhla.org.s3.amazonaws.com/22,03-Jul-1952.pdf.

7. *The Sunday School Builder*, October 1936.

8. Price, 58.

9. James T. Draper, Jr. with John Perry, *LifeWay Legacy*, (Nashville: B & H Books, 2006), 147.

10. *The Challenge*, August 17, 1930.

11. *The Sunday School Builder*, October 1936.

12. David Francis, *The 5 Step Formula for Sunday School Growth* (Nashville: LifeWay Press, 2005), 4.

13. "Arthur Flake, Sunday School Pioneer, Dies at Age of 90 in Memphis," *Baptist Press*, July 3, 1952, http://media.sbhla.org.s3.amazonaws.com/22,03-Jul-1952.pdf.

14. Letter from Arthur Flake to Dr. J. M. Frost on the letterhead of the Flake & Neilson Co., Cash Department Store, April 30, 1908.

15. Draper, 148.

16. Ibid.

17. Nathan Gunter, "Gaines S. Dobbins and Scientific Management Theory in 20th Century Church Education," *Christian Education Journal*, Vol. 12, No. 2, November 1, 2015, p. 356, https://journals.sagepub.com/doi/pdf/10.1177/073989131501200207.

18. "A Speech That Influenced the South," *The Sunday School Builder*, October 1936, 3.

19. Arthur Flake, "About the Author," *Building a Standard Sunday School*, rev. ed. (Nashville, TN: Convention Press, 1956).

20. Price, 61.

21. Arthur Flake, *Life at 80 As I See It*, (Nashville: Broadman Press, 1946), IV.

22. *The Sunday School Builder*, October 1936.

23. Charles S. Kelley, Jr., *Fuel the Fire* (Nashville: B & H Academic, 2018), 92.

24. Life at 80 As I See It, p.XII.

25. "Arthur Flake, Sunday School Pioneer, Dies at Age of 90 in Memphis," Baptist Press, July 3, 1952, http://media.sbhla.org.s3.amazonaws.com/22,03-Jul-1952.pdf.

26. Layman Develops Sunday School Plan, p. 16.

27. Kelley, 94.

28. Ibid, 18.

29. Arthur Flake, *Building a Standard Sunday School* (Nashville, The Sunday School Board of the Southern Baptist Convention, 1922), 21-40.

30. Ibid, 47-48.

31. Ibid, 45.

32. Ibid, 48-50.

33. Francis, David, *The 3D Sunday School* (Nashville, LifeWay Press, 2006), 8.

34. Steve Parr, *Sunday School That Really Responds* (Grand Rapids, Kregel Publications, 2011), 105.

35. Ibid, 91.

36. Ibid, 90-91. Parr writes, "You will not average 100 percent attendance, and this is not the aim of your Sunday school enrollment. The aim is to regularly minister to 100 percent of those enrolled, and if your church will do so while continuing to add others to the ministry lists (rolls), you are much more likely to experience growth than if you purge the rolls and minister to fewer people." (p. 91).

37. J.N. Barnette, *A Church Using its Sunday School* (Nashville, Convention Press, 1936), 18. Barnette, influenced heavily by Flake, wrote: "First, let it be said that a church can reach people—large numbers of people. However, people must be sought and won to regular attendance. Churches that wait for the people to come will be disappointed."

38. R. Othal Feather, *Outreach Evangelism Through the Sunday School* (Nashville, Convention Press, 1972), 31. Feather wrote: "Prospects for outreach evangelism through the Sunday School are persons who are not members of the local church. They are persons who have manifested some interest in spiritual guidance by enrolling for Bible study or allowing their children of youth and younger ages to enrol (sic) in the local Sunday School. In the author's experience, approximately one third of these persons are unsaved."

39. Arthur Flake, *Building a Standard Sunday School* (Nashville: Convention Press, 1922), 103.

40. J.N. Barnette, *A Church Using its Sunday School* (Nashville, Convention Press, 1936), 19. Barnette wrote: "In many situations, some 50 percent of the church members are not enrolled in Sunday school. A church will usually find a large list of prospects by checking the church roll against the Sunday school roll, thus securing the names of all the Church members not enrolled in Sunday school."

41. Arthur Flake, *Building a Standard Sunday School,* (Nashville: Convention Press, rev. ed. 1954), 27.

42. "Railroad Facts … Construction, Safety and More," *Saferack,* December 3, 2019, https://www.saferack.com/railroad-track-facts-construction-safety/.

43. Arthur Flake, *Building a Standard Sunday School,* rev. ed. (Nashville: Convention Press, 1956), 62.

44. J. Maureen Henderson, "Working on the Weekend Is the New Normal and That's a Bad Thing," *Forbes,* April 28, 2017, https://www.forbes.com/sites/jmaureenhenderson/2017/04/28/working-on-the-weekend-is-the-new-norm.

45. Bruce Raley & David Francis, Extreme Sunday School Challenge: Engaging Our World Through New Groups (Nashville: LifeWay Press, 2012) 38-42.

46. Ed Stetzer and Mike Dodson, *Comeback Churches: How 300 Churches Turned Around And Yours Can Too,* (Nashville: B & H Publishing, 2007) 148-149.

47. Arthur Flake, *Building a Standard Sunday School,* rev. ed. (Nashville: The Sunday School Board of the Southern Baptist Convention, 1954), 30.

48. Ibid, 30.

49. "The 80 Percent Rule: Fact or Fiction?" *Alban at Duke Divinity School,* https://alban.org/archive/the-80-percent-rule-fact-or-fiction/ and Gary Nicholson Blog, https://gnichol.wordpress.com/2016/06/17/the-80-percent-rule-myth-or-fact/.

50. David Francis, *The 5 Step Formula for Sunday School Growth* (Nashville: LifeWay Press, 2005), 9 https://s7d9.scene7.com/is/content/LifeWayChristianResources/5stepformula_fullbookletpdf.pdf.

51. Flake, Building a Standard Sunday School, rev. ed. (Nashville: Convention Press, 1956), 31.

52. Ibid, 60-63.

53. Ken Braddy, "8 Reasons Why Groups Should Use Curriculum," *Encouraging and Equipping Sunday School & Small Groups,* March 14, 2018, https://kenbraddy.com/2018/03/14/8-reasons-why-groups-should-use-curriculum/.

54. Dr. Charles S. Kelley, Jr., *Fuel The Fire, Lessons from the History of Southern Baptist Evangelism* (Nashville: B&H Academic, 2018), 91.

55. Ibid, 91-92.

56. Dr. James L. Garlow, *How God Saved Civilization* (Ventura, CA: Regal Books, 2000), 334.

57. Kelley, 94.

58. Arthur Flake, *The True Functions of the Sunday School,* rev. ed. (Nashville: The Sunday School Board of the Southern Baptist Convention, 1951), 64.

59. Arthur Flake, *Sunday School Officers and Their Work,* rev. ed. (Nashville: The Sunday School Board of the Southern Baptist Convention,1936), 20.

60. Ibid, 18.

61. Ibid, 30.

62. Ibid, 20.

63. *Annual of the Southern Baptist Convention 1934*, 301. Archives of the annual SBC book of reports can be viewed at http://www.sbhla.org/sbc_annuals/. The reports are for the preceding church year. For example, the 1909 report officially covers the period October 1907 through September 1908. However, since the reports are submitted in the spring prior to the annual meeting of the convention, more recent items are often submitted as if looking ahead.

64. *Annual of the Southern Baptist Convention 1919*, 249. http://sbhla.org/sbc_annuals/.

65. *Annual of the Southern Baptist Convention 1919*, 468. http://sbhla.org/sbc_annuals/.

66. *Annual of the Southern Baptist Convention 1920*, 450-451. http://sbhla.org/sbc_annuals/.

67. *Annual of the Southern Baptist Convention 1918*, 428-429. http://sbhla.org/sbc_annuals/.

68. *Annual of the Southern Baptist Convention 1929*, 356. http://sbhla.org/sbc_annuals/.

69. *Annual of the Southern Baptist Convention 1923*, 244. http://sbhla.org/sbc_annuals/.

70. *Annual of the Southern Baptist Convention 1936*, 286. http://sbhla.org/sbc_annuals/.

71. *Annual of the Southern Baptist Convention 1935*, 317. http://sbhla.org/sbc_annuals/.

72. *Annual of the Southern Baptist Convention 1932*, 329. http://sbhla.org/sbc_annuals/.

73. *Annual of the Southern Baptist Convention 1937*, 320. http://sbhla.org/sbc_annuals/.

74. *Annual of the Southern Baptist Convention 1936*, 289. http://sbhla.org/sbc_annuals/.

75. *Annual of the Southern Baptist Convention 1937*, 321. http://sbhla.org/sbc_annuals/.

76. Karina Reddy, "1920-1929," *Fashion History Timeline*, May 11, 2018, https://fashionhistory.fitnyc.edu/1920-1929/.

77. Geoff Williams, "A Glimpse at Your Expenses 100 Years Ago," *U.S. News & World Report Money*, Jan. 2, 2015, https://money.usnews.com/money/personal-finance/articles/2015/01/02/a-glimpse-at-your-expenses-100-years-ago.

78. Warren, Rick, *The Purpose Driven Church* (Grand Rapids, MI: Zondervan, 1995).

79. Parenthesis added by author to emphasize how we guard our soul from the enemy.

Authors

David Apple serves as the National Director of Consulting/ Training, CORE 7 (www.thecore7.net) and as Associate Pastor, Big Canoe Chapel, Big Canoe, GA.

Ken Braddy is LifeWay's Director of Sunday School and a 30-year veteran of church education ministries in the local church. He is a blogger, author, trainer, and Sunday School practitioner. kenbraddy. com

David Francis retired from LifeWay as Director of Sunday School in 2018. His books and accompanying training modules can be downloaded at LifeWay.com/DavidFrancis.

Bob Mayfield serves Oklahoma Baptists in the areas of personal evangelism and small groups. Bob previously served churches in Arizona and Texas as a minister of education. Twitter @bobmayfield; Facebook @thebobmayfield

Dwayne McCrary leads teams that create ongoing BIble study resources for LifeWay, is an adjunct professor at Midwestern Baptist Theological Seminary, and teaches ongoing Bible study groups in his church. Prior to coming to LifeWay he served churches in Texas and Tennessee. @gdwayne

Dr. Steve Parr is nationally known as an author, keynote speaker, practitioner, and advocate of church growth strategies. He currently serves as the Executive Director of Missions for Georgia's largest association of churches, the Gwinnett Metro Baptist Network. His signature book, Why They Stay is researched based and examines what keeps kids connected to churches into their adult lives. Learn more at www.steveparr.net.

Bruce Raley has served on church leadership teams in Arkansas, Florida and Tennessee. He also served as the Director of Education Ministries for LifeWay Christian Resources for ten years. Bruce has a passion for leadership development and the creation of new Bible study groups. He and Donna have been married since 1982. @bruceraley

Alan Raughton was Adult Ministry Specialist at LifeWay for over 24 years before moving back to the local church where he serves Nashville First Baptist Church, Nashville, Tennessee as Pastor of Christian Education and Discipleship. A sought-after Sunday School trainer and speaker, Alan has written and co-written three books on Sunday School in addition to numerous articles on Sunday School and church health.

Allan Taylor is the Executive Pastor of Ministries at First Baptist Church Concord in Knoxville, TN. He served previously as Director of Sunday School & Christian Education at LifeWay. He has written two books, *The Six Core Values of Sunday School* and *Sunday School in HD* along with four DVD Training series: *Sunday School Done Right, Forward From Here, A Sunday School Strategy That Works,* and *The Inspired Teacher.* He and Linda have three children and three grandchildren.

Addendum

Photo of Flake's Notes presenting outline of what became Chapter III and the only known written record of "Flake's Formula" in his handwriting.

Abridged text from *Building a Standard Sunday School* by Arthur Flake, Chapter III. Enlargement (Nashville: Convention Press, 1922) pages 19-40.

This section of the book was the first publishing of what would eventually become "Flake's Formula."

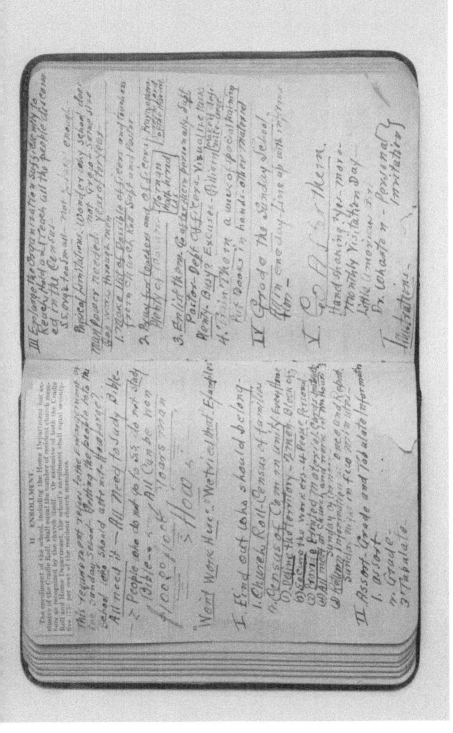

Enlargement

Standard requirement:

1. The enlargement of the school shall at least equal the number of resident church members as recognized by the church.

2. The school shall promote a program of visitation.

In checking on this requirement the first necessary information is the recognized *resident* church membership (not the total reported membership). To meet this requirement, the Sunday school enrolment, including the Cradle Roll and Extension departments, the general and department officers and teachers, shall at least be equal to the number of resident church members.

This is the only one of the ten requirements in the Standard of Excellence that refers directly to the subject of Sunday school enlargement. The other nine requirements deal with the school's efficiency; that is, with what the school should do for the pupil after he becomes a member.

Development in Sunday school growth is not confined to any particular locality or section of the country nor to any special types of Sunday schools. Rural churches, town churches, and city churches, both in "down-town" and residential sections, can experience a material increase in enrolment and in attendance when right methods of Sunday school building are employed.

Note a few examples:

A Sunday school in a country community had for years maintained an attendance of about sixty. It was graded and moved up from a class to a department pattern and at once began to grow and in a few months had a regular attendance of about two hundred.

A Sunday school in a small town, having a regular attendance of fifty, as a result of a training school culminating in a census, moved up to a department pattern. It began to take on new life and within a year was having a regular attendance of about three hundred.

A Sunday school in a large city had for twenty-five years maintained an attendance of around four hundred. Some proved, up-to-date methods were employed and within eighteen months the school was having a regular attendance of 1,500.

The explanation: *Vision, Study, Right Methods, and Work.*

Pastors and superintendents are fast realizing that we have just been playing at the Sunday school business from the standpoint of reaching people, and that a large Sunday school can be built wherever people live in large numbers.

There is inspiration in numbers, but let it be understood that a school does not necessarily have to have an enrolment of a thousand members to be great. It may be a really great school and have an attendance of a hundred or even less. However, no Sunday school is worthy of being called a great school unless it is reaching a large majority of the people who should attend it. This is true no matter what other claims to efficiency it may have.

The Standard of Excellence emphasizes this as a great principle underlying Sunday school work, and requires that a Sunday school must be reaching the people in a large way before being entitled to recognition as a Standard school.

The requirement that a Sunday school must have on its rolls a number equal to the resident church membership is not a difficult requirement. There is no good reason for a Sunday school anywhere not being able to meet this requirement if the proper methods are used.

I. THE CONSTITUENCY FOR THE SUNDAY SCHOOL SHOULD BE KNOWN

The constituency of the Sunday school can be secured from three sources, namely, the present Sunday school roll, the church roll, and the prospects found by taking a religious census of the community.

1. *Checking the Church Membership Roll*

Certainly every church member should be in Sunday school. Every church member should be studying the Bible. He should be studying the Bible with the other church members in the Sunday school. There is little definite Bible study done outside of the Sunday school, not enough to take into consideration, so we might say that people who do not go to Sunday school do not study the Bible.

The first source from which we begin building the attendance of the Sunday school is the membership of the church- the members should be in the Sunday school. Let the superintendent and pastor go carefully over the church roll, compare it with the Sunday school roll, and make a list of all those who do not attend the Sunday school.

2. *Taking A Religious Census*

A religious census should be taken at least annually in every community; in growing centers and communities, twice each year; and in mill and factory districts, with shifting, changing populations, a canvass may be needed every three months. The purpose of the census is to get information to be used in building the Sunday school. At the same time, it is a good way and worth while to let the people know that the Sunday school is at work and anxious to help in every way possible.

Either the pastor or the general superintendent should take charge and act as general director of the census, or some definite individual should be selected and enlisted for this work. The following steps should be taken to guarantee a successful house-to-house canvass and to make this, work most effective.

(1) *Defining the territory.*—The legitimate territory for which the church is responsible should be decided upon by the superintendent and pastor and any others they wish to consult. A specific definition of this territory will need to be given for the census. In cities, maps may be used and certain boundary streets or natural divisions can be found. In rural communities roads will serve.

(2) *Preparing the assignments.*—The preparation of the territory for assignment will need careful clerical attention by some who are familiar with it. There should be the general division into some four or more districts, according to size, using natural or assigned

dividing lines. If possible, have a good map of each district. Then each one of these districts should be subdivided into blocks or sections small enough to be canvassed by a worker in two hours' time. The number of these small divisions will, of course, determine how many census takers must be enlisted.

Each block or section should indicate how many houses are contained in it. Use a card, or secure an envelope for this purpose large enough to hold the census cards and draw an outline map of the territory on the front of the envelope. Follow the same general plan for towns and rural communities, using the natural dividing lines, roads, highways, etc., in preparing the territory.

(3) *Enlisting the workers.*—A capable individual should be selected and placed in charge of each of the larger districts as captain. His task would be to familiarize himself with his territory and at the proper time, when his workers are assigned to him, be ready quickly to assign the territory to them, get them out on the field, and assist them in any other way possible. He should not be responsible for enlisting the workers.

Then comes the task of actually enlisting the necessary census takers. One fine way is to assign a quota to each department, and, in the Young People's and Adult ages, to each class. Then lead them to work toward getting the quota actually signed on the dotted line .at least one week before the census is to be taken.

Each age group up through the Juniors should be asked for a quota equaling the number of officers and teachers. The fifteen- and sixteen-year-old Intermediates make fine workers if paired off with Adults.

The pastor will lay it upon the hearts of the people from the pulpit and the superintendent will do the same from the platform, but the task of securing the workers to do the canvassing must be done by personal solicitation, and urging will often be necessary. No effort should go unused and no slackening of energy should be allowed until sufficient census takers have been secured.

(4) *Providing sufficient materials.*—Many times the taking of a census is handicapped because of insufficient materials with which to work.

There should be a most liberal supply of census cards. Every home is to be entered and a card filled out for every individual. A shortage of materials here will prove disastrous. For the best results, do not change the card. The simpler it is and the fewer questions it carries, the easier will be the work and the more nearly complete the information secured.

Other materials will include a sufficient supply of pencils, rubber bands, and the census assignment envelopes carrying "Instructions to Census Takers."

(5) *Selecting the time and instructing the workers.*—Any season of the year is suitable, and any time a good time for this work. The best day in the week for the work in most cases is Sunday afternoon. It is the most suitable time as the people are at leisure and it is easier to get the required number of census takers.

In this day of Sunday afternoon outings it is far better to arrange to serve a light lunch in the church at the close of the morning service and send the census takers out by one o'clock. This will increase the effectiveness of the census at least a third. Otherwise, gather at the church as early in the afternoon as possible.

At the appointed hour gather the census takers together for a period of devotion and general instruction. Give each census taker a copy of "Instructions to Census Takers."

Three things will need especial emphasis at this meeting: First, let it be thoroughly understood that the workers must go into every home, talk with the people no matter who they are and get information concerning every body. Second, insist that a card should be made for each individual in the home. No one is to be omitted and no two are to be combined on one card. Third, make clear that every blank is to be filled. If any question is not answered the card may possibly have to be thrown away. Workers should not be allowed to take the census unless they attend the meeting for instructions, for they cannot be counted on nor expected to know how· to do this work correctly and efficiently.

(6) *Assigning the territory.*—The general instructions ought not to occupy more than fifteen minutes. The meeting should then break up into sections which should be presided over by the district captains, who should quickly assign to each worker the territory he is to canvas. Each captain should have a secretary to list the workers as they are assigned their territory and to see that each one is provided with a pencil and a liberal supply of census cards. Also each captain should have enough automobiles to send his workers out to their territory. Instruct them to bring all the cards back to the church as soon as their work is completed.

It is most helpful for the pastor at the Sunday evening preaching service to give a few minutes for verbal reports from the workers. Many short, helpful sermons will come from their experiences.

3. *Preparing the Information for Use*

The information as brought by the census takers and secured from the church roll is not by any means ready to be used and little lasting good will come from the work done unless it is put in convenient form to be used.

(1) *Assorting the information.*—All cards showing a preference for other denominations are thrown to themselves. All other information would belong to the church taking thc census. Included in this would be the membership of the church taking the census, all the members of their families, Baptists with membership else where, persons expressing preference for Baptist churches, and all those expressing no preference. All this information should be carefully checked against the church and Sunday school rolls so that a composite of the three sources of in format ion will be available and so that duplications can be eliminated.

(2) *Grading the information.*—The next step is to grade all the information gained from the church roll and the census. This should be done on the age group basis, as follows:

Cradle Roll and Nursery—birth through 3

Beginners—4, 5

Primaries—6, 7, 8

Juniors—9, 10, 11, 12

Intermediates—13, 14, 15, 16

Young People—17 through 24

Adults—25 and above

Extension—all who cannot attend Sunday school

All over eight years of age should be graded by sex as well as by age.

Where the possibilities for a Sunday school are large, the information will have to be graded closely. Often provision will have to be made for one or more department for each age below Young People's, with several classes for each age of boys and each age of girls in the Junior and Intermediate departments. In such cases there should be close grading for all Young People and Adults also. Separate classes and departments should be provided for married Young People. The information would determine how many classes there ought to be in each department. The classes for Beginners, Primaries, Juniors, and Intermediates should be kept small, not more than ten to each class, and even smaller.

(3) *Tabulating the information.*—The next thing after grading the information is to tabulate it. It should be typewritten and visitation assignments should be prepared. This is absolutely necessary if the best results are to be had. The census cards may be used as the basis for a permanent prospect file.

It is best, if the information is typewritten, to have at least five copies made, one each for the pastor, superintendent, department superintendent, and teacher, and one to be filed for future reference. Some schools have the information printed or mimeographed in order that each member may be furnished with a copy. In this way it is easier to keep a permanent record of the possibilities for the school.

It is well for a school to supplement these lists by as signing a few prospects to each teacher each week, with the understanding that they are to be visited by the class within the week. Reports of the visits will be turned in at the weekly officers and teachers' meeting.

II. The Organization Should Be Enlarged

It will be necessary to enlarge the organization in order to take care of all the people on the church roll and those discovered in the census. There will be no use to go on with the same old organization hoping to increase the size of the Sunday school permanently. Unless the present Sunday school organization is enlarged, practically all of the work done in taking the census will come to naught.

To be sure, a few people will join the Sunday school as a result of being visited during the census, but there can be no large permanent growth unless there is an organization strong enough to reach, hold, and teach the people who should be in the Sunday school. A church should provide at least one worker for every ten people it seeks to enroll in its Sunday school. The size of the organization needed is dictated by the number of pupils available, as revealed by the information secured.

Immediately this organization should be outlined and the leaders should set themselves to the enlistment of the necessary workers. Where will a Sunday school look for so many additional teachers? How will they be induced to take up the work? They are to be found within the membership of the church and nowhere else. If approached in the right manner they can be induced to serve. There are three steps which, if followed persistently, will produce the required number of officers and teachers:

1. *Praying Publicly and Privately for Workers*

Prayer is a proved method; Jesus used it. He prayed all night before choosing the twelve apostles. He commanded us to use it. He said, "Pray ye therefore the Lord of the harvest, that he will send forth labourers into his harvest" (Matt: 9: 38).

The task of choosing and enlisting these new officers and teachers for the Sunday school should be made a matter of prayer at all services. It should be made a subject of private prayer daily by the pastor, the superintendent, and all others who are interested. There is no undertaking which requires greater faith and more wisdom than this. (James 1:5-7)

2. Making a List of Prospective Officers and Teachers

The pastor and superintendent should carefully go over the church roll, name by name, and make a list of all the members possessing teaching gifts and qualities of leadership. A study of the church membership from this viewpoint will be illuminating and encouraging.

As the superintendent and pastor select from the church roll those who possess teaching gifts and qualifications, they should write their names into the new organization, adjusting each one to the place in which he is best suited to serve. Changes and readjustments will be necessary before the new organization is completed. Many delightful thrills will come to the pastor and superintendent as they study the church membership with reference to the ability of each one to serve in the Sunday school in some capacity.

3. Securing the Consent of Those Who Have Been Selected to Serve

It is surprising how men and women who love God will respond to a definite appeal to service. Many of the best men and women in all churches have done little in Christian service because they have never been offered an appealing task. To the question, "Why stand ye here all the day idle?" the answer comes back, "No man hath hired us." "We have no task—we do not know what to do."

The superintendent and pastor should hold personal interviews with all those who have been selected to serve, and urge them to accept the work assigned them. Visualize the task to all, lay it heavily upon their hearts and pray with them and for them. Show that man a list of eight boys fourteen years of age who need him to go after them and teach them and win them to Christ. Show that young woman seven girls ten years of age who need her—many of them not in the Sunday school, and perhaps not one of them knowing Christ. Do not take "no" for an answer. Be insistent. No Christian should allow any pretext to turn him aside, such as lack of time, pressing household duties, and similar age-old excuses. There are many capable young people in all the churches who love the Lord and really desire to serve him. They may be frivolous and merry and even worldly. Go after them. Lay upon their hearts their obligation to serve Christ. Win them away from the things they are doing by giving them a place where they may serve Christ. Do not give up. Get the teachers.

When they answer that they do not know how to teach, promise to give them the necessary help. This book and other books of the Sunday School Training Course should be put into the hands of each one of them. A training class should be organized and they should be led in a study of the book selected. The pastor, the superintendent, or someone else capable of doing so should teach this class. A functioning officers and teachers' meeting will offer effective in-service training. Find the teachers, enlist them, and train them.

III. A SUITABLE PLACE SHOULD BE PROVIDED

There is no such thing as building a Sunday school great in numbers in small, cramped quarters. Neither can a Sunday school of the highest efficiency be operated without proper equipment. While good equipment does not necessarily guarantee an efficient Sunday school, at the same time, it is necessary if a Sunday school is to do the best quality of work.

1. *Adjusting Present Quarters*

In planning to increase the growth of the Sunday school, it is often necessary to readjust the arrangements of the building. Often an Adult class is meeting in a large room when a much smaller room would serve its purpose. If properly approached the class can easily be induced to make the exchange and the large room may be utilized for taking care of an entire department with small classes. Other rooms may sometimes be divided by sound-proof partitions in such a way as to provide for more classes so that the teachers may work with greater effectiveness.

Frequently there is not half room enough in the present quarters. As a temporary arrangement it is sometimes wise to secure outside space. Perhaps a lodge room may be secured close by for the Junior or Intermediate department or for an Adult class. A public school building near by may be rented for one or more classes or entire departments. A tabernacle may be erected close by the church building to take care of one or more departments or one or more classes.

Again let it be said that a large Sunday school cannot be built and maintained in small, cramped quarters; and sane, sensible arrangements should be made for the expansion of the Sunday school. The building fixes the pattern for the Sunday school, sometimes for years to come.

2. *Erecting New Buildings*

Many Sunday schools have to "swarm" before the church membership realizes that a larger, better equipped building is needed. Hundreds and even thousands of our church houses in the Southern Baptist Convention territory are wholly inadequate from the standpoint of size and proper adjustment to take care of the Sunday schools the churches should have. In many of these situations, churches should erect new buildings, both from the standpoint of efficiency and economy. There is no economy in a church maintaining a small, inefficient Sunday school when there are multitudes of people all around who could be won if adequate quarters were provided. A church that takes care of its home base, all things being equal, will do more in the way of giving the gospel to those afar. The command from our Saviour is, you shall be witnesses unto me both in Jerusalem, and in all Judaea, and in Samaria, and unto the uttermost part of the earth."

IV. The Enlarged Organization Should Be Set Up

The Sunday following the religious census the new enlarged organization should be put into operation. The simplest and easiest way to do this is to grade the present Sunday school and assign the teachers to the pupils present; then put into the hands of the teacher of each class a list of all the pupils for whom he is responsible. Be sure no name is omitted. List all the pupils who are enrolled, plus all the prospective pupils secured from the church roll and discovered in the census.

Grading the Sunday school should be adopted by the church as its policy. It should receive the loyal support of all the officers and teachers. The reasons for grading should be made clear to all. When people have been properly prepared, it is easy to set up the needed departments and classes, with a clearly defined age range for each. In every age group, Adults included, Baptists have proved themselves ready to cooperate fully when they are led to understand the reasons for grading.

If the Six Point Record System is to be installed, a new classification of the entire school should be made, but care must be taken that no name is lost from the Sunday school roll.

When the new organization is set up, many teachers will have small classes to begin with, and perhaps some will not have any pupils at all. There should be placed in each teacher's hand the names of a sufficient number of prospective pupils to make a class when they are brought into the Sunday school. This is the condition which sends workers afield and produces Sunday school growth.

V. A Program of Visitation Should Be Maintained

The visitation of prospects and absentees is absolutely essential to the growth of any Sunday school. This is the last step in reaching the people and in constantly building up the membership and attendance of a Sunday school.

1. *A Program of Visitation*

As the matter now stands, during the enlargement campaign:

- *The church roll has been checked.*
- *The census has been taken.*
- *The information has been assorted, graded, and tabulated.*
- *The organization has been enlarged to take care of all the possibilities.*

- *The enlarged organization has been inaugurated. The proper space has been provided in the building.*
- *The information has been placed in the hands of the officers and teachers.*

If we stop here, all the work which has been done will be largely in vain, the organization will go to pieces and discouragement will result on every hand.

The thing needed now to enlarge the Sunday school is that this organization should be led by the superintendent and pastor to visit every one of the prospective pupils during the coming week and urge them to come to the Sunday school, and then keep visiting them from week to week with the same urgent invitation until all of them join.

At all times a sharp lookout for new pupils should be maintained by the heads of the departments, teachers, and pupils. All people moving into the community during the year should be located and visited as soon after their arrival as possible, and their names should be reported to the pastor and superintendent. The department superintendents and the class officers should be on the alert, going after the newcomers continually for their departments and classes.

As the Sunday school roll increases, the absentee list will also increase and it will be necessary for teachers and officers to visit absent pupils regularly week by week if they are to build them up in regular attendance.

Thus the visitation ministry of a school will assume large proportions and will demand constant attention. Regular weekly visitation should be accomplished, the assignments being made and the reports received at the weekly officers and teachers meeting. Special visitation times should be fostered for different groups. Individual visitation should be continuously urged and assignments made. All the ingenuity, skill and consecration of the leaders will be needed to plan a varied visitation program and inspire the workers constantly to participate in this all-important work. A definite plan of visitation is heartily recommended for all Sunday schools.

2. A Regular Visitation Day

If the best results are to come, a regular weekly or monthly visitation day should be observed. The main purpose of such a day is to visit the prospective pupils and to contact absentees.

(1) *The purpose of visitation day.*—The purpose of a regular visitation day is: First, to visit and urge all absent pupils to come back to the Sunday school; second, to visit the prospective pupils who have been discovered and urge them to become members of the Sunday school; third, to keep on the lookout for people moving into the community, locate them as soon after their arrival as possible, and report their names to the pastor and the superintendent.

A regular visitation day prayerfully and intelligently observed is almost a sure method of getting in touch with newcomers and will result in the return of absent pupils to the Sunday school. Often the list of prospective pupils secured in the census will be thoroughly worked up within a short time. A live list of prospective pupils may be secured for all the departments and classes by maintaining a well-planned and well-executed visitation day.

(2) *The best time to observe visitation day.*—In most cases Thursday is a satisfactory time for visitation day. It may be well to have the visitation for some age groups done during the day. Other age groups may be more effectively visited at night. A definite schedule should be set up and followed.

It is impossible to get a time that will suit and please all, but in the great majority of city and town schools, people can easily spend an hour or two regularly once a week visiting for the Lord. To be sure, some of the people will have to work and cannot go. However, if the matter is properly presented, it will be possible to get one or more representatives from each class to take part in the visitation.

Some Sunday schools select Saturday afternoon because it is a half holiday and the people in cities who work in offices, factories, shops, and other like places are at leisure, and are usually glad to give an hour to visiting. Again, Saturday afternoon has the advantage of proximity to Sunday, and may yield better results on this account.

Agree to have a regular visitation day, set a time for it, plan for it, observe it.

(3) *The plan for visitation day.*—Someone asked, "Why have a specified visitation day? Why not everybody visit when he can?" That is the very reason for setting aside a definite time to do Sunday school visiting. Everybody" doesn't visit "when he can." Remember this, people who do Sunday school visiting only when it is convenient, do not visit at all.

The value of having a plan for Sunday school visiting lies largely in the fact that people will visit in groups and not alone. For this reason the Sunday school ought to agree to have a regular visitation day, select the time that will suit the largest number, and observe it. The pastor should make frequent references to it from the pulpit and it should be given as much publicity as possible.

The direction of the whole matter necessarily should be in the hands of the general superintendent. He should be the guiding spirit and see to it that the day is planned for regularly. However, the planning and visiting can be done best by departments. Each department superintendent would naturally direct the work of visiting in his department. He can do whatever planning is necessary with his teachers at the weekly officers and teachers' meeting. Of course, each teacher should also visit his own pupils and prospects at other times.

Nothing should be left to chance. A sufficient number of automobiles should be secured and the routings of each arranged. Promptly at the specified time all who are to engage in the visitation should meet at the church building. The department superintendents should quickly get their officers and teachers together and assign them their visiting lists and send them out with as little delay as possible.

First, every pupil who was absent the previous Sunday should be visited and earnestly urged to be in his place the following Sunday.

Second, group leaders should plan with their group members to visit their absentees and the one or two prospects assigned to the group.

Third, every teacher should have a list of prospective pupils who should be visited and lovingly invited to join the Sunday school.

The Six Point Record System offers forms for making visitation assignments and reporting the results. The use of these forms will point out the purpose of the visit and so help train the visitors. Making a report in writing serves to keep the information in the church files up to date. It also trains the visitor to summarize and evaluate his visit and often furnishes an incentive for a further visit.

(4) *The ones who should do the visiting.*—The pastor and superintendent should frequently go. Usually they would be on the lookout for new teachers; they should also call on the sick and those in trouble. If for no other reason, they should go for the influence of their example.

The department superintendents should lead the teachers and pupils in their departments, being sure that no one is overlooked who should be visited. Sometimes a department superintendent may have to do the visiting for one or more of his teachers who could not possibly go. Often he will visit with an inexperienced teacher. Every teacher who can possibly arrange to go should avail himself of the opportunity offered by visitation day to visit his absent pupils. He should also gain new recruits for his class from the list of prospects furnished him. This is the teacher's best chance to build the class. Group leaders of Young People's and Adult classes should enlist their groups to join enthusiastically in this campaign. They should go in groups under the direction of the group leader.

Junior and Intermediate pupils will be glad to join their teachers and will enjoy greatly the work of visiting. A regular visitation day offers an opportunity to Intermediate and Junior teachers to utilize and interest their pupils and enlist them in real service.

A teacher of an Intermediate class of girls had the regular members of her class meet at her home and go to the church in a body. One of the girls was heard to remark that she was "just crazy about Sunday school visiting."

Several members of a class of Intermediate boys of ten members, not one of whom had been absent for a month, met, at the suggestion of their teacher, and helped other classes with their visitation.

The Cradle Roll superintendent and her workers will find the regular visitation day a delightful time to visit in the interest of the Cradle Roll. Birthday cards and other materials can be delivered to the homes and many new babies enrolled in the Cradle Roll department.

The Extension department superintendent and visitors can also take advantage of this opportunity, delivering literature and looking out for new members for this department.

(5) *The benefits of a regular visitation day.*—The Sunday school will grow in numbers. This is certain. The one unfailing method of reaching new pupils for the Sunday school and bringing back the absentees is the personal visit. People will join the Sunday school if they are asked. It is not nearly so difficult to reach people for the Sunday school as we imagine. It is far more difficult to get members of the Sunday school to visit them. The absentee list of any Sunday school can be reduced by fifty to seventy-five percent if the absentees are contacted each week and sufficiently urged to return to the school.

Through visitation the officers and teachers of the Sunday school come into personal touch with the pupils in their homes and places of business, and they can thus plan the more intelligently to meet their needs. Often the cooperation of parents is secured in this way and a correct solution of the problems confronting many of the pupils reached. On the other hand, when the parents of pupils are totally indifferent to their spiritual wellbeing, a knowledge of this condition will help the teacher in meeting his pupils' needs.

The pastor gains valuable information of his entire field through the Sunday school officers and teachers. The visitors should make written reports to the pastor of all cases really needing his attention.

The teachers have an opportunity to enlist their pupils in definite service. Both teachers and pupils will become more intensely interested in the school and in other people as they experience the joys which come through visiting. As they carry blessings into the homes and lives of those whom they visit, they too are blessed.

The Sunday school will be supplied with new material for building the school. New people moving into the community are quickly discovered by the visitors. The annual census is not sufficient, as in growing towns and centers people are moving in all during the year.

Going after people personally is the one unfailing method of reaching them for the Sunday school. Jesus gave us this method of how to get people into the Sunday school in the parable of the supper in the fourteenth chapter of Luke: "The master of the house ... said to his servant, ... Go out into the highways and hedges, and compel them to come in, that my house may be filled."

This method of going after people was good two thousand years ago and is just as good today. It is good in the city and good in the country. It gets results everywhere, every time. All other methods of reaching people for the Sunday school grow old and ineffective. This method of going after people personally never grows old, but is ever new, attractive, and resultful.

QUESTIONS FOR REVIEW

1. Mention the first step in reaching the people for the Sunday school. From what sources may the information be secured?

2. Why should the Sunday school organization be enlarged?

3. Give three steps necessary in securing the needed number of officers and teachers.

4. What should be done to provide additional room for the enlarged organization?

5. What is the next step in conserving what has been done? Name at least three methods for doing this.

6. State the threefold purpose of a regular visitation day. What is the plan for visitation day?